JUST THE WAY I SEE IT

PALMETTO
PUBLISHING
Charleston, SC
www.PalmettoPublishing.com

Just the Way I See It
Copyright © 2024 by Jonathan Carver

First Edition

Paperback ISBN: 979-8-8229-2900-5

Just the Way I See It

A LOOK INTO THE BOOK
OF THE REVELATION

Jonathan Carver

Contents

The Revelation to John
Commentary

Let me start by saying, that I am deeply humbled at the request of fellow members and worshipers of Christ that have asked me to write this Commentary. A few years ago, someone sent out a couple of surveys through some churches. One survey, asking members what book they would most like to hear taught, and the other asking ministers or teachers which book they would least like to teach? The number one answer to both surveys was the same "The Revelation." Why is that? Why do so many (myself included) stray away from this book?

I believe there are multiple reasons for both sides to feel the way that they do. First, the minister side, I feel that many avoid this book under the concern that not understanding it as a whole, however it is not necessary to understand everything in this book to profit from it! John says that it is a great benefit, just to hear this book read. Also, having so many alternate beliefs from the book, all that are available, leaves teachers "choosing sides" and not just teaching the Bible. On the opposite side, hearers are both wanting someone to explain to them, the things that they struggle to understand, or refuse to study for themselves. Some just seek answers, and often to questions that have no definite conclusion spelled out in black and white. Finally, I believe for both sides that, the hearer wants to know answers, and good Bible teachers, well, they are afraid without complete understanding that they will not have the correct answers.

Having said all of that, let me encourage you to take time to read the book of The Revelation yourself, to study yourself. When you come to something that you don't understand, or that you don't know. Keep reading, don't guess, and for heavens sakes don't quit! Again, you do not have to understand everything that is being seen, heard, or spoken of to gain spiritual insight or growth. Let me also take this time to speak to why I personally feel that The Revelation is a concern for understanding.

We love a good story, a definite plot, a hero, a villain, victory and loss, failure and God pulling someone through. We love a good character or object study, what all someone accomplished and lost in their life, or how many victories that the Ark of the Covenant helped win for Israel. Now, in the 404 verses that are in The Revelation, there are hundreds and hundreds of references into the Bible! Mainly, into the old testament, and more so into Psalms, Isaiah, Ezekiel, and Daniel. All of those books are full of great information that John, reminds us of or is reminded of by the angels. The problem? If we are checking character studies, or object studies, we are not reading, Psalms, Isaiah, Ezekiel, or Daniel (well not past chapter 6 anyway). That leaves us feeling as though everything in Revelation is new, or has been top secret all of our lives. But, allow me to remind you that the God of the Universe who gave this Revelation to John, and also told him to write it down. He is that same one that allowed his son to come and die for our sins! He isn't trying to fool his children, he isn't throwing a curve late in the game! He loves you and has filled it with information, to remind you that He has been in charge throughout this world, and Victory is His. So us? Well, if we want to be victorious, then we must be as Joshua with the Captain of the Lords Host and recognize that we must be on God's side!

Chapter 1

1:1 The Revelation of Jesus Christ, which God gave unto him, to shew unto his servants things which must shortly come to pass; and he sent and signified it by his angel unto his servant John:

1:2 Who bare record of the word of God, and of the testimony of Jesus Christ, and of all things that he saw.

1:3 Blessed is he that readeth, and they that hear the words of this prophecy, and keep those things which are written therein: for the time is at hand.

As we are introduced into the greeting of the book, John starts us at the beginning, and is careful to let us know that this is not what was "his revelation" but it was Christ's Revelation. It is not something that was given to John over anyone else but shown to John so that others may know. Think for a moment about the Gospels in the New Testament. All telling one story, with different viewpoints and for different groups and reasons. Now, imagine if multiple people from their views tried to tell this story? Instead, we will see that John was chosen and shown this Revelation from all points, and even as some consider this confusing, this gives us a flow through the book. It provides for us a continual line of communication for all, that we may also know this Revelation of Christ. John is clear in verse two to let us know that he includes all things that he saw, and in verse three to share that there are blessings associated with this Revelation. Would you expect anything different, than Christ providing for his people blessings, and encouragement?

1:4 John to the seven churches which are in Asia: Grace be unto you, and peace, from him which is, and which was, and which is to come; and from the seven Spirits which are before his throne;

It is important to note here that these are not the only seven churches in Asia at the time of this letter. It is unclear (to me anyway) why these were the chosen churches, but what is clear is that the messages to them were to be shared and inform all churches. Both, those in Asia and the churches that were yet to come, that Christ died for us to be reconciled wholly unto him, and not partially as we to often live.

1:5 And from Jesus Christ, who is the faithful witness, and the first begotten of the dead, and the prince of the kings of the earth. Unto him that loved us, and washed us from our sins in his own blood,

While there have been thousands of witnesses unto the work of reconciliation with God, Christ is the only one who has walked in *flesh on this earth and been faithful! In all things he was faithful to the Father, he was faithful to the work of the cross, and he was faithful to us a believers in never leaving nor forsaking one of us. It is Christ who was the first resurrection from the dead. I know some are asking what about the widow's son, or the man thrown on the bones of Elisha? What about Lazarus? Those all required an external source, in obedience to God for completion! Christ's resurrection required no external source, but was a reminder unto the entire world, that Christ as He said had power to lay his life down, and power to raise it up again. Through that we too shall be raised through the same power of Christ that overcame the hold and power of Death and Hell.*

1:6 And hath made us kings and priests unto God and his Father; to him be glory and dominion for ever and ever. Amen.

Because of his resurrection Christ has made, don't miss that, MADE! us as believers the Kingdom of God. This isn't something that he is going to do, or that Revelation reveals is going to happen, but instead remind us of when this took place.

1:7 Behold, he cometh with clouds; and every eye shall see him, and they also which pierced him: and all kindreds of the earth shall wail because of him. Even so, Amen.

1:8 I am Alpha and Omega, the beginning and the ending, saith the Lord, which is, and which was, and which is to come, the Almighty.

As we read verse seven and eight, there is a reminder that Christ is not hiding his supreme work on the cross. It is important I believe to point out here the God has never hidden his work, yet it was Judas with Satan in him that was under the cover of night hiding his betrayal. It was Satan under the cover of a serpent, hiding his deception. That said, it can be deemed then that the work of Revelation that we read is not a first for God trying to hide or prevent us from knowing him! He is the Almighty, He was the Almighty, and He is coming as the Almighty!!

1:9 I John, who also am your brother, and companion in tribulation, and in the kingdom and patience of Jesus Christ, was in the isle that is called Patmos, for the word of God, and for the testimony of Jesus Christ.

John takes a moment to remind us that he is not an elite human, but he is our brother, he is our friend in tribulations. He is our friend in the kingdom of God, and he is all of those thing's thanks to the patience Jesus had in his life. The same as we are because of the patience that Christ has had in ours.

1:10 I was in the Spirit on the Lord's day, and heard behind me a great voice, as of a trumpet,

John was in the only place he could have been for Christ to come to him, he was in worship, as the Bible teaches us to be in Spirit and in Truth.

1:11 Saying, I am Alpha and Omega, the first and the last: and, What thou seest, write in a book, and send it unto the seven churches which are in Asia; unto Ephesus, and unto Smyrna, and unto Pergamos, and unto Thyatira, and unto Sardis, and unto Philadelphia, and unto Laodicea.

1:12 And I turned to see the voice that spake with me. And being turned, I saw seven golden candlesticks;

1:13 And in the midst of the seven candlesticks one like unto the Son of man, clothed with a garment down to the foot, and girt about the paps with a golden girdle.

1:14 His head and his hairs were white like wool, as white as snow; and his eyes were as a flame of fire;

1:15 And his feet like unto fine brass, as if they burned in a furnace; and his voice as the sound of many waters.

1:16 And he had in his right hand seven stars: and out of his mouth went a sharp twoedged sword: and his countenance was as the sun shineth in his strength.

Christ speaks to John, and when he turns his eyes catch first the candlesticks, and then in the midst of them as so many other encounters with individuals seeing Christ, was one like unto the Son of man. A reminder again that when Christ speaks into our lives, there is no doubt of his direction, or purpose for his coming to us. The visual of the Son of man, speaks to his position and follows what we read that we are to be like through the scriptures.

His garment draped with a Golden girdle to signify his royalty and place as King of Kings, the hair white reminding us of wisdom and truth. The flaming eyes, the burn through the wood, hay, and stubble, as well as purifying the gold and precious stones that we are to build our lives with. His feet as the gospel of truth, here pure and fine, just as the Gospel is simple and true, yet elegant and strong. His voice as the sound of many waters, deafening and drowning all doubt just as He did with Peter walking on the water that night. The stars in his hand we will see shows the angels obedience to him, and the sword of his tongue cutting to the marrow of our bones. His face as bright as the sun shining in full strength, reminds us of Moses' encounter to see God's glory, and from his hind quarters needing a veil to cover the brightness. No wonder evil will be slain at the brightness of his coming, not only in his return, but as we invite him into our lives and He pushes back the darkness of sin and defeat in our lives.

1:17 And when I saw him, I fell at his feet as dead. And he laid his right hand upon me, saying unto me, Fear not; I am the first and the last:

Is it not amazing that Christ's response to John collapsing was in knowing that it wasn't the brightness, or unbelievable sight that got John. It was the fear or being in the presence of the One Righteous Lord, who simply comforted John with his hand as he does us so many times and said to him; Fear Not! Take heart beliver that in Christ alone we have nothing to fear, He is for us!

1:18 I am he that liveth, and was dead; and, behold, I am alive for evermore, Amen; and have the keys of hell and of death.

1:19 Write the things which thou hast seen, and the things which are, and the things which shall be hereafter;

1:20 The mystery of the seven stars which thou sawest in my right hand, and the seven golden candlesticks. The seven stars are the angels of the seven churches: and the seven candlesticks which thou sawest are the seven churches.

Here we are told the mystery that was the stars and the candlesticks. The Candlesticks being the churches, and the stars the angels of those churches. Remember what angels are as Hebrews tells us "are they not ministering spirits" and here also they are for the purpose of ministering to the churches. What can we take from this? That just as it is today for us, before we can be made aware of what Christ has for us we as these 7 churches over the next two chapters, have to receive the ministry of God and correct our wrongs. Then and only then can the rest of this Revelation be presented before them. Only then for us also can understanding begin to take place in our lives as we strive to live for Christ.

Chapter 2

For the next two chapters, instead of verse by verse, I will break at the end of each letter to the churches with notes and fill in.

2:1 Unto the angel of the church of Ephesus write; These things saith he that holdeth the seven stars in his right hand, who walketh in the midst of the seven golden candlesticks;

2:2 I know thy works, and thy labour, and thy patience, and how thou canst not bear them which are evil: and thou hast tried them which say they are apostles, and are not, and hast found them liars:

2:3 And hast borne, and hast patience, and for my name's sake hast laboured, and hast not fainted.

2:4 Nevertheless I have somewhat against thee, because thou hast left thy first love.

2:5 Remember therefore from whence thou art fallen, and repent, and do the first works; or else I will come unto thee quickly, and will remove thy candlestick out of his place, except thou repent.

2:6 But this thou hast, that thou hatest the deeds of the Nicolaitanes, which I also hate.

2:7 He that hath an ear, let him hear what the Spirit saith unto the churches; To him that overcometh will I give to eat of the tree of life, which is in the midst of the paradise of God.

We find the beginning of Ephesus in Acts chapter 18 and can follow some of its growth thru chapter 20. Some years later we can read that they were growing and doing well in Paul's letter to the Ephesians. It is in Timothy chapter 1: 3-7 that we begin to see some of their falling as Paul encourages Timothy to stay there and "charge them to teach no other doctrine." Saying also in verse 7 of Timothy chapter 1 that they were "desiring to be teachers of the law; understanding neither what they say, nor whereof they affirm."

Now in Revelation, John is told to write to them from, he that holdeth the seven stars in his right hand, who walketh in the midst of the seven golden candlesticks; Christ is reminding Ephesus that He holds the power of their ministry in His hand, and that he is walking in the midst of all of His Churches. Telling Ephesus that this is not something someone has reported to Christ, but Christ in the presence of Ephesus has seen these things Himself. Let us also be reminded that no one has to tattle to Christ about our Church, or our actions, He still remains in the midst and hold accountable His Church to the completion of the Gospel. It is easy to jump and say that they have left Christ altogether in this passage, but I would ask this; what is the first love of a believer? While Christ is not a bad choice for an answer here, it was the Gospel which first in power and spirit revealed to us our place. It was the Gospel of Christ the didn't leave us in that position, yet offered hope through accepting Christ and His work on the cross. Placing here the argument that a believers first love would be the complete Gospel of Christ, which opened our hearts to sin, and offered at the same time a way out of that sin. Ephesus is still full of good works, patience, standing against evil, laboring and not fainting. They have not left Salvation, or the recognition of Christ, but have left the preaching of the entire Gospel. Willing instead to make compromise, so some don't feel left out, or so the sting of sin feels less than what it is. We see it in churches today where they are willing to say Jesus can fill your life, or Christ will forgive all, but leaving out what a detriment sin is, and that there is judgement for the wrong in our lives. Let us not stray from the complete Gospel message! Let us who have also repent, remember and repent as Christ has said here.

2:8 And unto the angel of the church in Smyrna write; These things saith the first and the last, which was dead, and is alive;

2:9 I know thy works, and tribulation, and poverty, (but thou art rich) and I know the blasphemy of them which say they are Jews, and are not, but are the synagogue of Satan.

2:10 Fear none of those things which thou shalt suffer: behold, the devil shall cast some of you into prison, that ye may be tried; and ye shall have tribulation ten days: be thou faithful unto death, and I will give thee a crown of life.

2:11 He that hath an ear, let him hear what the Spirit saith unto the churches; He that overcometh shall not be hurt of the second death.

There is not mention of the church of Smyrna, being 35 miles north of Ephesus, it is believed to have been established around Acts chapter 19 while Paul was in Ephesus. Here Christ comes to Smyrna as the first and the last, which was dead, and is alive; which I feel plays an important role in what Christ is saying to the church. There are no faults in Smyrna that are listed for us to read about, just as Pilate said of Christ (I find no fault in this man). Smyrna is translated into Myrrh, the herb that was used as perfume for the living, and preservation of the dead. For the scent of myrrh to be of effect the herb must be crushed, beaten, and ground to release the scent that is desired. The same holds true for the church, as they have been under blasphemies, sufferings, and pain. Christ reminds them to be as he was, faithful even unto death, and they shall receive the crown of life. Finishing up by telling them that, overcoming the pain and sufferings of this life, will lead to not being hurt by the second death.

What does that mean for us? That we need to realize that it doesn't take wrong doing to bring on suffering. If that were the case Christ would have never suffered while he was earth. That the church should continue to expect persecution, just as Christ received while he was here. Hold fast to the unchanging hand of the Lord, and we to shall not fear the second death.

2:12 And to the angel of the church in Pergamos write; These things saith he which hath the sharp sword with two edges;

2:13 I know thy works, and where thou dwellest, even where Satan's seat is: and thou holdest fast my name, and hast not denied my faith, even in those days wherein Antipas was my faithful martyr, who was slain among you, where Satan dwelleth.

2:14 But I have a few things against thee, because thou hast there them that hold the doctrine of Balaam, who taught Balac to cast a stumblingblock before the children of Israel, to eat things sacrificed unto idols, and to commit fornication.

2:15 So hast thou also them that hold the doctrine of the Nicolaitanes, which thing I hate.

2:16 Repent; or else I will come unto thee quickly, and will fight against them with the sword of my mouth.

2:17 He that hath an ear, let him hear what the Spirit saith unto the churches; To him that overcometh will I give to eat of the hidden manna, and will give him a white stone, and in the stone a new name written, which no man knoweth saving he that receiveth it.

Here in Pergamos, John writes and portrayed Christ again in a different way; this time He is he which hath the sharp sword with two edges;. Written to a church that had a major problem ongoing. Pergamos is placed in a tough position, where the majority of the population was not believers, and where pagans continued to press their ways on the church. (Sadly sounding a lot like our beloved USA) Yet, Pergamos has not gave up, nor have they denied their faith in Christ. So, what is it that they have done? Why is Christ presenting himself as the sharp two edged sword? Christ said I recognize your position, that you are in a land filled with unbelievers, worshippers of Baal, which have caused a problem in Pergamos. The Church while not denying their faith in Christ, have tried to divide their faith. No longer allowing God to be their complete provision, they have held to their form of worship, yet to appease the larger religion, have made allowances to accepting food offered before false gods, and fornication. They are working to be a church led by Christ, yet one that is accepted of all the world around them. We were not called to be accepted, but to be separated showing a dark world the light of a marvelous Christ. Now, here comes the two edged sword, Christ says to them, cut yourself loose from the world that you are trying to appease. If you fail to repent and cut yourself loose, Christ says, I will come and fight against them with my two edged sword. Christ will not accept a mingle of worship, and commitment we must sell out completely to him. Only in complete separation from the world, can we find the provision of Christ. Here he is reminding them of something he told his disciples, I have bread that ye know not of, and only in separation can we find this through Christ.

2:18 And unto the angel of the church in Thyatira write; These things saith the Son of God, who hath his eyes like unto a flame of fire, and his feet are like fine brass;

2:19 I know thy works, and charity, and service, and faith, and thy patience, and thy works; and the last to be more than the first.

2:20 Notwithstanding I have a few things against thee, because thou sufferest that woman Jezebel, which calleth herself a prophetess, to teach and to seduce my servants to commit fornication, and to eat things sacrificed unto idols.

2:21 And I gave her space to repent of her fornication; and she repented not.

2:22 Behold, I will cast her into a bed, and them that commit adultery with her into great tribulation, except they repent of their deeds.

2:23 And I will kill her children with death; and all the churches shall know that I am he which searcheth the reins and hearts: and I will give unto every one of you according to your works.

2:24 But unto you I say, and unto the rest in Thyatira, as many as have not this doctrine, and which have not known the depths of Satan, as they speak; I will put upon you none other burden.

2:25 But that which ye have already hold fast till I come.

2:26 And he that overcometh, and keepeth my works unto the end, to him will I give power over the nations:

2:27 And he shall rule them with a rod of iron; as the vessels of a potter shall they be broken to shivers: even as I received of my Father.

2:28 And I will give him the morning star.

2:29 He that hath an ear, let him hear what the Spirit saith unto the churches.

Keeping with description this time it is the eyes of flaming fire, and feet of fine brass. The church is known to Christ for their works, charity, service, patience, and again their works; with the latter works more then the first. There is very little told about the church in Thyatira, but we have heard of them before. Be reminded of a lady named Lydia in Acts chapter 16, the one who was a seller of purple. That is some insight to the city, as it was also a trade city.

The church was a working church, one that not only spoke of doing, but was also putting into action working for Christ. It is the only church that was spoken of for the love that it had for people. Know for service in the community, and being patient with the world around it. Finally, the works again, this time more than the first; in other words they were not resting on what had been done in the church, but continued to press and work for Christ. So, what did they do wrong? Ephesus was a church that had solid doctrine, and failed to love others. Thyatira, is that in opposite, they are "loving" so much that they are willing to sacrifice doctrine, in the name of love for others. The question to be raised, is love without truth ever love? Would it be loving to never teach right for fear of hurt, or would it be as Solomon said in Proverbs the one who spares the rod (correction) hateth the child? Solomon said, not correcting a child in the name of love (or anything else for that matter) is actually no love at all. There is where the downfall comes for this church.

Christ said " thou sufferest that woman Jezebel" some believe and say this is an actual woman in the city. I ask simply who would name their daughter Jezebel? It would be like naming a child Hitler today, or Lucifer. Instead I feel it is a reference to the one and only Jezebel that married King Ahab. Now, not that he was much of a king to start, but immediately he changed to worship of Baal. A quick plug here to remind your children growing up to be cautious in choosing their mate, your spouse will make or in this case break you! Jezebel, ushered in false worship, hatred, idolatry, and a complete turning from God. Much the same here, Thyatira, has suffered (tolerated) these sins and it has leaked into the church.

This has came in with a combination of love without doctrine, and toleration. Make no mistake about this, if you tolerate something, you will eventually accept it as normal, or begin to *practice it yourself. So, what were they tolerating? Again, this is a trade city, and all trade if regulated by, what are known as guilds. These guilds come in and take over aspects of trade, and brought sinful acts along with them. In this case acts of fornication, and idolatry. Now, if a guild says you can not buy or sell, then that was the end of the case; and what was happening in this situation. So, here comes the toleration, church members saying things like, if I don't accept this worship, then I will loose my job. Making excuses along the lines of, well, I am only doing it for my family; I mean we have to eat and live right? I go to the fornication gatherings, but, I don't get involved, and I teach my children that its wrong. Actions are louder than words, and teaching friends. A pastor of mine growing up always said it this way, If I make moonshine and sell it, my kids, will make it, sell it, and drink it. Their kids, will make, sell, drink, and abuse it.*

Christ's appearance to the church here, is a reminder that he sees all that is going on. Now, while we as people, may make excuses and tolerate things, we are warned it is detrimental to us as well. We should never tolerate the intolerable, regardless of what the cost, don't forget where your provision comes from. Christ, said I see what is going on, and I am going to stop it. He let's us know that he has given room and place for repentance, and Jezebel has refused. That she calls herself a prophetess, no one else does, and Christ certainly will not, but he says. I am going to throw her on a bed of tribulation, and all those who refuse to repent with her. This is not the nice haired, lowly Jesus that we are accustomed to seeing, but it is one that we need to know and reverence. He will not put up with our tolerance of sin, anymore than he did in Thyatira.

There were still some who had not given in, they were taking the loss if you will of worldliness, and keeping with the truth. To these he makes a promise. One of no other burden, for keeping right. One that says if you will hang on till the end, he will endue them with power over the nations. Not in the manner of ruling them, but seeing them broken for their sins. He references himself being broken by the Father! Let's stop here a moment and reflect on the happening on the cross, where God not only allowed his Son to be broken for our sin, but God was the one that had to do the breaking! There is the forsaking, Christ called out about on the cross. He knew it was coming, but that did not mean he wanted it, or enjoyed it. His love for us was just far greater than the pain and death. Then Jesus said to those I will give the morning star,

A quick note on the morning start as we end this discussion. Lucifer was once referenced as the morning stat in Isaiah, and some question that here. Lucifer, or Satan, as has been referred to as a lion seeking whom he may devour. Peter referenced Jesus as the morning star as well, so how do we differ the two? Isaiah was speaking of Lucifer as the angel, and it is told he was the most beautiful and bright, the issue for Lucifer as the morning star, was his light was created and given to him. It also, burnt out, just as a start the literally falls from the heavens now burn out. He no longer reflects the light of the Father. Christ on the other hand even through death, did not rely on anyone else for his light *source, the Bible still says there is no night in that city, for He is the light! He is the ever burning Bright and Morning Star. More to come on the lion comparison later.*

Chapter 3

3:1 And unto the angel of the church in Sardis write; These things saith he that hath the seven Spirits of God, and the seven stars; I know thy works, that thou hast a name that thou livest, and art dead.

3:2 Be watchful, and strengthen the things which remain, that are ready to die: for I have not found thy works perfect before God.

3:3 Remember therefore how thou hast received and heard, and hold fast, and repent. If therefore thou shalt not watch, I will come on thee as a thief, and thou shalt not know what hour I will come upon thee.

3:4 Thou hast a few names even in Sardis which have not defiled their garments; and they shall walk with me in white: for they are worthy.

3:5 He that overcometh, the same shall be clothed in white raiment; and I will not blot out his name out of the book of life, but I will confess his name before my Father, and before his angels.

3:6 He that hath an ear, let him hear what the Spirit saith unto the churches.

As Thyatira was the longest letter and lengthy in discussion, so shall Sardis be one of the shortest of both as well. As with all things concerning Christ, do not let the length fool you, as this is equally important. Christ appears as "He that hath the seven Spirits of God, and the seven stars;" He says only one thing to Sardis, "I know thy works, that thou hast a name that thou livest, and art dead." I can't help but think that nothing more saddening could be said to a church. They think they are alive, the world around them believes that they are alive, but they are dead. In Matthew 23:27, Jesus said this of the Pharisees, that they had beautiful garments, but on the inside were full of dead mens bones. Paul, also made mention of the same in 2 Timothy 3:5, as he warned Timothy to stay away from such "having a form or godliness, but denying the power thereof: from such turn away."

They were not always dead, as they have garments, but they are soiled. While we are not told what has brought this death on the church, we are told the remedy. Sometimes, we get to affixed on the problem, and not the solution. (I am not trying to be mean spirited, or cold hearted in saying this.) Does cause of death really matter to a family in the moment that a loved one is lost? Jesus, does not take time to walk thru the cause of death, instead instantly says the cure. Remember, what you have received and heard and hold fast to it. Once you have remembered, repent! To many believers, know they aren't living right, know they should do better, and know what they have been taught. To many, also stop there, in saying I know I need to do better or more, but Jesus said that is the first step, not the last! The last is repentance, and if we fail to repent, Jesus will come on us when we are not expecting and require of us an answer.

Finally, Christ reminds them, that all is not lost. There are some there in Sardis that are still alive, some that still have white garments that have not been soiled. He also, reminds those who have soiled garments, that with repentance, they can again be white. That he would in fact, confess their name before his Father! Don't live life as if you are ready for a funeral. Don't be dressed right, with no life in you, instead repent and live as Christ has called us all to.

3:7 And to the angel of the church in Philadelphia write; These things saith he that is holy, he that is true, he that hath the key of David, he that openeth, and no man shutteth; and shutteth, and no man openeth;

3:8 I know thy works: behold, I have set before thee an open door, and no man can shut it: for thou hast a little strength, and hast kept my word, and hast not denied my name.

3:9 Behold, I will make them of the synagogue of Satan, which say they are Jews, and are not, but do lie; behold, I will make them to come and worship before thy feet, and to know that I have loved thee.

3:10 Because thou hast kept the word of my patience, I also will keep thee from the hour of temptation, which shall come upon all the world, to try them that dwell upon the earth.

3:11 Behold, I come quickly: hold that fast which thou hast, that no man take thy crown.

3:12 Him that overcometh will I make a pillar in the temple of my God, and he shall go no more out: and I will write upon him the name of my God, and the name of the city of my God, which is new Jerusalem, which cometh down out of heaven from my God: and I will write upon him my new name.

3:13 He that hath an ear, let him hear what the Spirit saith unto the churches.

Stationed on the largest trade route out of Rome, we can see why Christ would speak to Philadelphia about open doors. What greater place could a church as for, than to be a stopping point on the way for weary travelers? Nothing was said against the church of Philadelphia, and while we are so use to reading about failures being addressed in these letters. We are reminded that Christ does not only send correction, He also brings uplifting encouragement to believers. History says in reference to the synagogue of Satan, that about 10 miles out of town there was remains found with engravings pointing toward that being the building. People, would often come to Philadelphia, and lie about their status as a believer, but the church was patient to continue holding the true Gospel up. In doing that Christ took note, and Christ still takes note to-day of churches that refuse to water the truth of Christ's death and resurrection being the only source of redemption and forgiveness.

The pillar in a temple, is thought to reference the location again, as it was a place of many earthquakes. So many in fact that the church was destroyed multiple times in quakes, and had to be rebuilt. Christ is saying to remain strong and overcome, and in doing so he will make the believer a pillar in new Jerusalem. A solid continual place, where they can worship forever, without fear or destruction.

3:14 And unto the angel of the church of the Laodiceans write; These things saith the Amen, the faithful and true witness, the beginning of the creation of God;

3:15 I know thy works, that thou art neither cold nor hot: I would thou wert cold or hot.

3:16 So then because thou art lukewarm, and neither cold nor hot, I will spue thee out of my mouth.

3:17 Because thou sayest, I am rich, and increased with goods, and have need of nothing; and knowest not that thou art wretched, and miserable, and poor, and blind, and naked:

3:18 I counsel thee to buy of me gold tried in the fire, that thou mayest be rich; and white raiment, that thou mayest be clothed, and that the shame of thy nakedness do not appear; and anoint thine eyes with eyesalve, that thou mayest see.

3:19 As many as I love, I rebuke and chasten: be zealous therefore, and repent.

3:20 Behold, I stand at the door, and knock: if any man hear my voice, and open the door, I will come in to him, and will sup with him, and he with me.

3:21 To him that overcometh will I grant to sit with me in my throne, even as I also overcame, and am set down with my Father in his throne.

3:22 He that hath an ear, let him hear what the Spirit saith unto the churches.

The old saying last, but not least as we come to the church of the Laodiceans is certainly one that comes to mind. Christ comes as the Amen, the faithful and true witness, the beginning of the creation of God. Amen, to let it be, or to be in agreement with. The faithful and true witness, not just any witness, Christ is the only true witness. The only one that has seen and knows the way things are in heaven, as well as the earth. The beginning of the creation of God, this is to me an interesting proclamation. When we think of the creation we think of light, darkness, earth, water, and man. We think of Adam, and his sin in the garden; but what we don't often think of is this. When creation began, it began with God, the perfect triune being, and here if there was ever doubt is evidence that Christ too was at the beginning of creation.

It has been said many times that being hot or cold is a reference to living a Christian life. When we are praying, reading, and witnessing we are hot. When we are lazy, full of bitterness, or just skipping out on communication with Christ, we are then cold. I can completely understand this take on this section, but do not feel that is what Christ was saying. No where else in the scripture does Christ, that died for our forgiveness, desire that we would be cold. He does not want us to not pray, not read the Bible, or not seek him. I will hit the high points here on Laodicea, as to keep this somewhat brief and not drag along. The city is located in a place that seemingly has everything that would be needed, everything that is except water. All the water in the city was piped in from two neighboring cities, Colossae, and Hierapolis. Hot water for medicinal purposes from Hierapolis, and cold water from Colossae as drinking water. The issue is that with the nearest being 5 miles away, whether hot or cold at the source, the water came into Laodicea lukewarm. Christ I believe is telling the church that, they are neither cold and refreshing, nor hot and healing to anyone. The Church is in a state of lukewarmness and has need to move itself closer to the source, Christ.

What causes lukewarmness in our lives? Here we see Christ references that the Church has came to a place, where it is "self sufficient." No Church should ever desire self sufficiency, rather the stronger a church desires to be, the more dependency that must take place in the church. The greater our independence grows, the farther we move from the source, and we become neither refreshing to one another, nor healing to sinners. That is why in verse eighteen, Christ counsels the church to buy of Him. To fully rely

on his provision, and not rest on the ability that they have to pro-
vide a way of life for themselves.

Why the Amen? Why the faithful and true witness, and the
beginning of the creation of God? We see that answer take shape
in verse twenty, as Christ says to the church in nineteen to repent,
and then Behold, I stand at the door, and knock: This is import-
ant as a reminder to a church that had became self reliant, as it
makes this point. Christ does everything for us! It is not that we
make the right move, or right decision. It isn't that we walk twen-
ty miles, to get to Christ. Nay, but that we recognize the need for
repentance that he calls us to, and in that moment; knock, knock,
knock. He is there, calling and pleading with us to fully depend
on him! He is there, you don't have to travel to achieve his pres-
ence! He is there, because the work of the cross remains sufficient
today, and nothing more is needed to bring you into his presence.

Chapter 4

Revelation 4:1 After this I looked, and, behold, a door was opened in heaven: and the first voice which I heard was as it were of a trumpet talking with me; which said, Come up hither, and I will shew thee things which must be hereafter.

Revelation 4:2 And immediately I was in the spirit: and, behold, a throne was set in heaven, and one sat on the throne.

To this point, John has written and told us that he was on the Isle of Patmos, Christ has appeared to him, and asked him to write. He wrote to the Churches, and here in Chapter four, there is a great change. Not a change of information, not a change of speaker, but a change of perspective. John is not looking at what is about to take place over the next seventeen chapters from the Isle of Patmos, but is being moved, we too must move out of worldly position and thought as we consider the remainder of The Revelation.

Revelation 4:3 And he that sat was to look upon like a jasper and a sardine stone: and there was a rainbow round about the throne, in sight like unto an emerald.

Revelation 4:4 And round about the throne were four and twenty seats: and upon the seats I saw four and twenty elders sitting, clothed in white raiment; and they had on their heads crowns of gold.

Notice the clothing of the elders, they are in white raiment, just as Christ has promised through the letters in chapters two and three. What John has written about he is now seeing for himself to be true.

Revelation 4:5 And out of the throne proceeded lightnings and thunderings and voices: and there were seven lamps of fire burning before the throne, which are the seven Spirits of God.

Lets take a moment here to breathe, there is a lot taking place here as John enters the open door. One is setting on the throne, colors are everywhere, and everything is being counted. We are going to see a lot of numbers through the remainder of the book, and here is a small break down. One is Unity/God; Seven is Divine perfection throughout the Bible, twelve is Perfection in a governmental sense. Four is a reference towards Earth, Five is Grace, and Six is man/sin.

Revelation 4:6 And before the throne there was a sea of glass like unto crystal: and in the midst of the throne, and round about the throne, were four beasts full of eyes before and behind.

Revelation 4:7 And the first beast was like a lion, and the second beast like a calf, and the third beast had a face as a man, and the fourth beast was like a flying eagle.

Revelation 4:8 And the four beasts had each of them six wings about him; and they were full of eyes within: and they rest not day and night, saying, Holy, holy, holy, LORD God Almighty, which was, and is, and is to come.

All of these four (earth) beasts, have earthly characteristics in verse seven, then in verse eight we find the six wings. A flashback to Isaiah, with the Seraphims that were crying to God in the Temple. Eyes all around reminding us that nothing, neither in Heaver or Earth has gone without being seen and noted by God.

Revelation 4:9 And when those beasts give glory and honour and thanks to him that sat on the throne, who liveth for ever and ever,

Revelation 4:10 The four and twenty elders fall down before him that sat on the throne, and worship him that liveth for ever and ever, and cast their crowns before the throne, saying,

Revelation 4:11 Thou art worthy, O Lord, to receive glory and honour and power: for thou hast created all things, and for thy pleasure they are and were created.

As the beasts are continually, crying out Holy, Holy, Holy unto the Lord God Almighty, the elders are continually falling before him on the throne, to worship and present their crowns

before him. These crowns are spoken of throughout the Bible, and here a show what takes place. Presenting them before God, is a reminder that without God, they would never have the crown in the first place. Also, it is a reminder that there is only one King of King, and Lord or Lords.

In this new perspective, the first thing that we see with it is an entrance to worship God, who is seated on his Throne. Some would automatically jump to this being something that is taking place in the future, but I would have to disagree. This worship has been taking place for some time and continues now, today, in this moment, Glory and Honor are being offered up before the Throne of God. As we continue to live and seek God's will here, let us be reminded of a line from the model prayer, Thy will be done in earth, as it is in Heaven. Not as it will be someday, but as it currently is, in heaven.

Chapter 5

Revelation 5:1 And I saw in the right hand of him that sat on the throne a book written within and on the backside, sealed with seven seals.

A minute here to pause and explain something about this writing, that it is one in which, we are looking at everything as symbolism, unless told otherwise. Some would say that everything is literal in this book of The Revelation, and should be viewed as symbols only when told to do so. Here is one instance of why I personally feel it is the other way, God is a Spirit, and if we are taking everything literal unless told otherwise, then here we have a Spirit with a literal hand. The issue there is, that spirits do not have human body parts, remember we have to change perspective from earthly. Also, if Spirits we built the same as humans, Christ would not have had the need to take on Human form, he could have just came and lived on earth as he was.

Revelation 5:2 And I saw a strong angel proclaiming with a loud voice, Who is worthy to open the book, and to loose the seals thereof?

What is it about this book, or scroll if you will? The Angel makes it clear that it will take someone special, not to open it, but to be worthy to open it. Think of it this way, being willing to redeem someone from their sins, does not make us worthy to be able to do so. Being able to hit a jump shot, does not make one worthy to play basketball at the highest level. So, the Angel is able to open the scroll, but is not worthy, the elders could have opened it, but are not worthy. What makes one worthy?

Revelation 5:3 And no man in heaven, nor in earth, neither under the earth, was able to open the book, neither to look thereon.

Revelation 5:4 And I wept much, because no man was found worthy to open and to read the book, neither to look thereon.

Wailing would be a good way to put the weeping that John is talking about in this verse, John is completely broken that no one can open this scroll. What makes it so important? That answer comes as we find one worthy to open the scroll.

Revelation 5:5 And one of the elders saith unto me, Weep not: behold, the Lion of the tribe of Juda, the Root of David, hath prevailed to open the book, and to loose the seven seals thereof.

Is it not fitting that an old saint, comforts John, calms him, and says Weep not? Just as through out lives so many times it is a tried and true servant that brings comfort to us in our dark moments.

Now for some thoughts on the previous questions. What is it about this scroll? Well, for starters it is written within and without, (two sided if you will) and this is rare for documents. It is even more rare for a document to have this many seals. Seven of them, divine perfection is taking place in what is about to be opened. Documents sealed this much, and written this way, narrows the options down, and leaves us with the possible answer of a living will and testament. Only an executor of the will could open it, and that executor is named the Lion of the tribe of Judah.

Why is it so important of a document that John is weeping, with none found to open it? So often again, we are futuristic minded with this Book, I would like to offer a thought to you that is a bit different. We will see in a moment in verse nine, that a new song was sung, a song about a lamb, and redemption. I don't feel John has looked into the future, but the past, and is seeing the work of Christ coming to present his sacrifice before God. That in realizing this time and position, John weeps, because without the opening of the scroll, there is no completion of Christ's work. The death of Christ in sacrifice, must be completed in offering it before God, and no one is worthy to read this will before the Throne. Then the Lion is revealed worthy to read it, but the Lion never takes the scroll, it is the LAMB that was slain that takes it. Showing to us that they are one and the same. More on the Lamb, and the importance of reading this scroll, over the next verses.

Revelation 5:6 And I beheld, and, lo, in the midst of the throne and of the four beasts, and in the midst of the elders, stood a Lamb as it had been slain, having seven horns and seven eyes, which are the seven Spirits of God sent forth into all the earth.

The position of the Lamb described here is important, in my determining the timeframe we are in. Is the Lamb on the throne? Is the Lamb among the Beasts? Or even as the one of the Elders? The answer to all is the same, no not really. He is around all of the above, but not an actual part of any. Hebrews tells us that Christ when He had gave Himself a sacrifice for all once, sat down at the right hand of the Father. That isn't where He is, instead He is showing that He is worthy to be among the believers, as well as among the Throne. Yet, has not completed his work to take his place on the Throne.

Revelation 5:7 And he came and took the book out of the right hand of him that sat upon the throne.

Again, a reminder that the Lion and the Lamb are one in the same.

Revelation 5:8 And when he had taken the book, the four beasts and four and twenty elders fell down before the Lamb, having every one of them harps, and golden vials full of odours, which are the prayers of saints.

Revelation 5:9 And they sung a new song, saying, Thou art worthy to take the book, and to open the seals thereof: for thou wast slain, and hast redeemed us to God by thy blood out of every kindred, and tongue, and people, and nation;

Revelation 5:10 And hast made us unto our God kings and priests: and we shall reign on the earth.

Thou art worthy to take the book, for thou wast slain. That comes from verse nine, John said as he looked and saw the Lamb, that it was a Lamb as if it had been slain. You will see as we continue through this study, that we will see Christ many times, but take note, this is the last time you will see him as if he was slain. Again, I feel it is that time between the crucifixion and presentation of his sacrifice to God the Father. And that, is what had John weeping! He had walked with Christ, He had seen the miracles, and knew the promises. He was at the Cross, and knows that the veil has been torn. He knows that in Christ's death, redemption and victory has been promised and He has held true to that. Now, he is seeing this before his eyes, Christ's last will that through him none should perish, but have everlasting life. Without this last will of Christ being presented before the Father, John knows his fate, and the fate of the world is doomed, and he Weeps. Now, as Paul once said, to know Christ and the POWER of HIS RES-URRECTION! We see that in the beginning, as the slain Lamb, walks to take His own last will from the Father and open the seals of it, so that it can be read and made known to the world. To this point, the worship of God has been present in Heaven, but that is all about to change as the Lamb takes the scroll! The heavens know, the world is about to know (resurrection from earth), Sa-

tan is about to know (as he is currently rejoicing in the victory he thinks he has won.) This rejoicing begins in this chapter in Heaven as the thousands and thousands of angels are about to kick off the rejoicing that is the Resurrected Saviour of the World.

Revelation 5:11 And I beheld, and I heard the voice of many angels round about the throne and the beasts and the elders: and the number of them was ten thousand times ten thousand, and thousands of thousands;

Revelation 5:12 Saying with a loud voice, Worthy is the Lamb that was slain to receive power, and riches, and wisdom, and strength, and honour, and glory, and blessing.

Revelation 5:13 And every creature which is in heaven, and on the earth, and under the earth, and such as are in the sea, and all that are in them, heard I saying, Blessing, and honour, and glory, and power, be unto him that sitteth upon the throne, and unto the Lamb for ever and ever.

Revelation 5:14 And the four beasts said, Amen. And the four and twenty elders fell down and worshipped him that liveth for ever and ever.

Chapter 6

Revelation 6:1 And I saw when the Lamb opened one of the seals, and I heard, as it were the noise of thunder, one of the four beasts saying, Come and see.

Revelation 6:2 And I saw, and behold a white horse: and he that sat on him had a bow; and a crown was given unto him: and he went forth conquering, and to conquer.

Revelation 6:3 And when he had opened the second seal, I heard the second beast say, Come and see.

Revelation 6:4 And there went out another horse that was red: and power was given to him that sat thereon to take peace from the earth, and that they should kill one another: and there was given unto him a great sword.

Revelation 6:5 And when he had opened the third seal, I heard the third beast say, Come and see. And I beheld, and lo a black horse; and he that sat on him had a pair of balances in his hand.

Revelation 6:6 And I heard a voice in the midst of the four beasts say, A measure of wheat for a penny, and three measures of barley for a penny; and see thou hurt not the oil and the wine.

Revelation 6:7 And when he had opened the fourth seal, I heard the voice of the fourth beast say, Come and see.

Revelation 6:8 And I looked, and behold a pale horse: and his name that sat on him was Death, and Hell followed with him. And power was given unto them over the fourth part of the earth, to kill with sword, and with hunger, and with death, and with the beasts of the earth.

Revelation 6:9 And when he had opened the fifth seal, I saw under the altar the souls of them that were slain for the word of God, and for the testimony which they held:

Revelation 6:10 And they cried with a loud voice, saying, How long, O Lord, holy and true, dost thou not judge and avenge our blood on them that dwell on the earth?

Revelation 6:11 And white robes were given unto every one of them; and it was said unto them, that they should rest yet for a little season, until their fellowservants also and their brethren, that should be killed as they were, should be fulfilled.

Revelation 6:12 And I beheld when he had opened the sixth seal, and, lo, there was a great earthquake; and the sun became black as sackcloth of hair, and the moon became as blood;

Revelation 6:13 And the stars of heaven fell unto the earth, even as a fig tree casteth her untimely figs, when she is shaken of a mighty wind.

Revelation 6:14 And the heaven departed as a scroll when it is rolled together; and every mountain and island were moved out of their places.

Revelation 6:15 And the kings of the earth, and the great men, and the rich men, and the chief captains, and the mighty men, and every bondman, and every free man, hid themselves in the dens and in the rocks of the mountains;

Revelation 6:16 And said to the mountains and rocks, Fall on us, and hide us from the face of him that sitteth on the throne, and from the wrath of the Lamb:

Revelation 6:17 For the great day of his wrath is come; and who shall be able to stand?

As I sit here tonight praying and working through this, I am reminded of the popularity in which the first 4 seals carry. People everywhere can talk about the White, Black, Red, and Pale horses, about their riders, debating who they are and what they mean. Don't cheat, here but what was the 5th seal? How about the 6th? You just read it 3 verses ago... Isn't it amazing how we put importance on certain aspects of the scripture, and so little on the rest? I mean all these are being opened in sequence, just Bam, Bam, Bam and we settle on horses and skip Saints praying, and the earth being shaken so that all in it cry for the rocks and mountains to hide them from Him that sitteth on the Throne, and from the wrath of the Lamb!

This is often referred to as the time frame of the end, after the church has been removed and the unbelievers remain. I have a question or two about that, and they come from the 5th and 6th seals. I am going to ask those for you to ponder as well, and then we will move to Chapter 7.

If this is the case and we are following Christ removing the church, why are there still souls of them slain for the word, and for their testimony. If we recall 1 Thessalonians 4, Paul reminds us that we will not prevent them which are asleep, that just as Christ arose bodily so shall we. If the timeframe of post resurrection is where we are, why are the souls still souls? Why are they still under the Throne and not freed to live and reign with Christ?

Furthermore, why are men calling for rocks to hide them from the wrath of God and the Lamb, if the horses and riders are in that end time as is so often said? Then the final question which leads us into Chapter 7 is asked in verse 17. For the great day of wrath is come, and who shall be able to stand? This is leading us in the direction to see that this is not occurring post end time, but pre end time leading up to the day that is to come. Now Chapter 7 and Who shall be able to stand?

Chapter 7

Revelation 7:1 And after these things I saw four angels standing on the four corners of the earth, holding the four winds of the earth, that the wind should not blow on the earth, nor on the sea, nor on any tree.

Revelation 7:2 And I saw another angel ascending from the east, having the seal of the living God: and he cried with a loud voice to the four angels, to whom it was given to hurt the earth and the sea,

Revelation 7:3 Saying, Hurt not the earth, neither the sea, nor the trees, till we have sealed the servants of our God in their foreheads.

Revelation 7:4 And I heard the number of them which were sealed: and there were sealed an hundred and forty and four thousand of all the tribes of the children of Israel.

Take notice in the first few verses here, the difference in the senses that are being used by John. He Saw, four angels, he saw, another angel, and then he hears the number of those that were sealed. I know many take this number literally, and they have the choice to

believe as they choose the same as I. But, let me put 144,000 into some perspective if I can. An estimated 6 million plus Jews were killed in the Holocaust between 1941 and 1945, that is 0.024% of the 6 million that were killed. Now we are talking about a complete number of Jewish people in 2020 around 15.2 million! That my friends, if we take this number literally is 0.009%!! In America alone, there are 210 million professed Christians, we are talking about living currently (well in 2021). I am not saying John heard wrong at all, I am saying (in my opinion) we are believing wrong. Let me explain more as to why as we look at this list from John.

Revelation 7:5 Of the tribe of Juda were sealed twelve thousand. Of the tribe of Reuben were sealed twelve thousand. Of the tribe of Gad were sealed twelve thousand.

Revelation 7:6 Of the tribe of Aser were sealed twelve thousand. Of the tribe of Nephthalim were sealed twelve thousand. Of the tribe of Manasses were sealed twelve thousand.

Revelation 7:7 Of the tribe of Simeon were sealed twelve thousand. Of the tribe of Levi were sealed twelve thousand. Of the tribe of Issachar were sealed twelve thousand.

Revelation 7:8 Of the tribe of Zabulon were sealed twelve thousand. Of the tribe of Joseph were sealed twelve thousand. Of the tribe of Benjamin were sealed twelve thousand.

This is the only place in the Bible that you will find this list, I know that there are several lists, throughout the Bible, and that many contain the 12 Sons/tribes of Israel. The thing is, all the other lists either only list the sons, or only lists the tribes. Now, John is a follower of Christ, and from what we have read and gathered just in this Revelation, he is an intelligent one at that. Mixing up this list is not something he did by mistake, not to mention let's remember who is showing and telling him this, is none other than Christ! While some could be either way here are the flags if you will, Manasses, would have been tribes not sons, yet Joseph and Levi would have been a list of sons and not tribes. This for me leaves the question of, if there is a literal 144,000 Jews to be sealed, where are they actually going to come from? They can't come from Tribes that didn't exist, and if we are going with Tribes, what about Ephraim? Joseph's tribe was divided between his two sons remember.

Revelation 7:9 After this I beheld, and, lo, a great multitude, which no man could number, of all nations, and kindreds, and people, and tongues, stood before the throne, and before the Lamb, clothed with white robes, and palms in their hands;

Revelation 7:10 And cried with a loud voice, saying, Salvation to our God which sitteth upon the throne, and unto the Lamb.

Revelation 7:11 And all the angels stood round about the throne, and about the elders and the four beasts, and fell before the throne on their faces, and worshipped God,

Revelation 7:12 Saying, Amen: Blessing, and glory, and wisdom, and thanksgiving, and honour, and power, and might, be unto our God for ever and ever. Amen.

Revelation 7:13 And one of the elders answered, saying unto me, What are these which are arrayed in white robes? and whence came they?

Revelation 7:14 And I said unto him, Sir, thou knowest. And he said to me, These are they which came out of great tribulation, and have washed their robes, and made them white in the blood of the Lamb.

Revelation 7:15 Therefore are they before the throne of God, and serve him day and night in his temple: and he that sitteth on the throne shall dwell among them.

Revelation 7:16 They shall hunger no more, neither thirst any more; neither shall the sun light on them, nor any heat.

Revelation 7:17 For the Lamb which is in the midst of the throne shall feed them, and shall lead them unto living fountains of waters: and God shall wipe away all tears from their eyes.

Now, that we have discussed, with more questions than answers, I am sure, the things which John heard. Let's move on and once again look at something he beheld (or saw.) A number, a multitude, not a "great Multitude" one that no man can number of every nation, every people, every language, crying Salvation to Our God that sitteth upon the Throne, and to the Lamb! I don't know about you, but it is seeming that we are passing through time, from a nation of God's people to a sacrifice sufficient to bring all Nation's under the Living God! Watch the Angels and all around the Throne that we have looked at so far, when the cry comes out of their mouths, they can only humble and bow their heads, and join in with AMEN! Blessing, and glory, and wisdom, and thanksgiving, and honor, and power, and might; be unto our God for ever and ever! When all of Heaven is joining in, it must be the Redeemed of God, it must be his people, it has to be God's Children. Now, who are they? John is asked and replies with thou knowest, and the word tribulation comes up. Many are looking for a great tribulation time, a time without the church, without Christ, a godless time. I would argue that a godless time would not be a great tribulation, but well we will see in just a few chapters Hell! The important part none the less, is to be assured, you are in that countless number, knowing the sacrifice of the Lamb, believing on the Son of God, and crying out praise to the God on the Throne and the Lamb!

Chapter 8

Revelation 8:1 And when he had opened the seventh seal, there was silence in heaven about the space of half an hour.

Revelation 8:2 And I saw the seven angels which stood before God; and to them were given seven trumpets.

Revelation 8:3 And another angel came and stood at the altar, having a golden censer; and there was given unto him much incense, that he should offer it with the prayers of all saints upon the golden altar which was before the throne.

Revelation 8:4 And the smoke of the incense, which came with the prayers of the saints, ascended up before God out of the angel's hand.

Revelation 8:5 And the angel took the censer, and filled it with fire of the altar, and cast it into the earth: and there were voices, and thunderings, and lightnings, and an earthquake.

Revelation 8:6 And the seven angels which had the seven trumpets prepared themselves to sound.

Revelation 8:7 The first angel sounded, and there followed hail and fire mingled with blood, and they were cast upon the earth: and the third part of trees was burnt up, and all green grass was burnt up.

Revelation 8:8 And the second angel sounded, and as it were a great mountain burning with fire was cast into the sea: and the third part of the sea became blood;

Revelation 8:9 And the third part of the creatures which were in the sea, and had life, died; and the third part of the ships were destroyed.

Revelation 8:10 And the third angel sounded, and there fell a great star from heaven, burning as it were a lamp, and it fell upon the third part of the rivers, and upon the fountains of waters;

Revelation 8:11 And the name of the star is called Wormwood: and the third part of the waters became wormwood; and many men died of the waters, because they were made bitter.

Revelation 8:12 And the fourth angel sounded, and the third part of the sun was smitten, and the third part of the moon, and the third part of the stars; so as the third part of them was darkened, and the day shone not for a third part of it, and the night likewise.

Revelation 8:13 And I beheld, and heard an angel flying through the midst of heaven, saying with a loud voice, Woe, woe, woe, to the inhabiters of the earth by reason of the other voices of the trumpet of the three angels, which are yet to sound!

Finally, the last Seal is being opened and we get, Silence. About half an hour no one speaks, no one is moving, just silence. Nothing else, is told to us about this seal otherwise, and then John sees Seven angels at the Throne of God, receiving seven trumpets to sound. Look a second at the smoke of the incense, rising before God, we find in the Levitical law that this is what took place with a sacrifice being accepted of God. Not until the prayers are lifted before God, does any action begin to take place in this chapter. Immediately, we want to start looking at these things happening in the fields and in the sky, and why not? Thunder and Lightning take place there, and fields are where the grass will wither, etc. Don't forget in the Book of Revelation, that things on the earth take place the same, we are still not wrestling against flesh and blood, but powers and principalities. Venture with me for a minute here, what if, just what if instead of literal withering and lightening, God is answering the prayers of the Saints. We are getting a look into the time and take notice that the Censer of burning coals was tossed into the Earth before any trumpets began to blow. I think it is clearer here that God was preparing the earth for trumpets and letting us see, that there has never been a time that He was not in control. Before evil, had a chance to sit foot on

God's creation, he had prepared a spiritual army for battle. He knew, what was about to happen at the sounds of these trumpets, as evil descended, and we will see in the beginning of Chapter 9 that Satan himself is being put out. The 1/3 that we read about here are the followers and those sided with him, God put them out before he ever dealt with Lucifer himself. Quick takeaway here, is that all the evil in your life will one day leave you standing alone as well, and you have no defense in the presence of an almighty and Holy God. Then we get a Woe cried out from the Heavens for the inhabiters of the Earth, evil is already raging and the last had not yet been sent down. Again, I don't believe we are looking at something coming to happen, for this earth is full of evil and raging already, but we are getting a look back showing us for certain that God has never not been in control of His creation.

Chapter 9

Revelation 9:1 And the fifth angel sounded, and I saw a star fall from heaven unto the earth: and to him was given the key of the bottomless pit.

Revelation 9:2 And he opened the bottomless pit; and there arose a smoke out of the pit, as the smoke of a great furnace; and the sun and the air were darkened by reason of the smoke of the pit.

Revelation 9:3 And there came out of the smoke locusts upon the earth: and unto them was given power, as the scorpions of the earth have power.

Revelation 9:4 And it was commanded them that they should not hurt the grass of the earth, neither any green thing, neither any tree; but only those men which have not the seal of God in their foreheads.

Revelation 9:5 And to them it was given that they should not kill them, but that they should be tormented five months: and their torment was as the torment of a scorpion, when he striketh a man.

Revelation 9:6 And in those days shall men seek death, and shall not find it; and shall desire to die, and death shall flee from them.

Revelation 9:7 And the shapes of the locusts were like unto horses prepared unto battle; and on their heads were as it were crowns like gold, and their faces were as the faces of men.

Revelation 9:8 And they had hair as the hair of women, and their teeth were as the teeth of lions.

Revelation 9:9 And they had breastplates, as it were breastplates of iron; and the sound of their wings was as the sound of chariots of many horses running to battle.

Revelation 9:10 And they had tails like unto scorpions, and there were stings in their tails: and their power was to hurt men five months.

Revelation 9:11 And they had a king over them, which is the angel of the bottomless pit, whose name in the Hebrew tongue is Abaddon, but in the Greek tongue hath his name Apollyon.

Revelation 9:12 One woe is past; and, behold, there come two woes more hereafter.

Revelation 9:13 And the sixth angel sounded, and I heard a voice from the four horns of the golden altar which is before God,

Revelation 9:14 Saying to the sixth angel which had the trumpet, Loose the four angels which are bound in the great river Euphrates.

Revelation 9:15 And the four angels were loosed, which were prepared for an hour, and a day, and a month, and a year, for to slay the third part of men.

Revelation 9:16 And the number of the army of the horsemen were two hundred thousand thousand: and I heard the number of them.

Revelation 9:17 And thus I saw the horses in the vision, and them that sat on them, having breastplates of fire, and of jacinth, and brimstone: and the heads of the horses were as the heads of lions; and out of their mouths issued fire and smoke and brimstone.

Revelation 9:18 By these three was the third part of men killed, by the fire, and by the smoke, and by the brimstone, which issued out of their mouths.

Revelation 9:19 For their power is in their mouth, and in their tails: for their tails were like unto serpents, and had heads, and with them they do hurt.

Revelation 9:20 And the rest of the men which were not killed by these plagues yet repented not of the works of their hands, that they should not worship devils, and idols of gold, and silver, and brass, and stone, and of wood: which neither can see, nor hear, nor walk:

Revelation 9:21 Neither repented they of their murders, nor of their sorceries, nor of their fornication, nor of their thefts.

Now as I said earlier here, we see a second star falling from Heaven, this one more powerful than that one called, Wormwood. This one has the key to the bottomless pit, a pit of destruction. See my friend, once you start down a path of disobedience, or walking away from God, there is not an end to the relentless punishment that one can endure. Satan is a raging lion we are told and looking for anyone he can devour. Devour is not to harm, or even to kill, but the entirely do away with. He without hesitation, opens this bottomless pit of disaster, smoke rolls out, and here come locusts like figures, with scorpion tails, and long hair, described in many various ways. While I have never seen such a figure, I believe we have all encountered them at some point, as we look at them briefly ask yourself what sin looks like. Bodies of horses, faces of men, crowns of victory, beautiful hair. Has gaining prestige in this life ever tempted you? The beauty of a woman? More strength and power as a great stallion? Yet, behind all of these is the same result, a tail with a stinger to hurt a man 5 months. No one has ever gone into anything in life looking to be injured or die. Drug addicts never woke up one day and said I am going to ruin my life; Sex addicts never woke up and said watch me throw away what I have. But all have been stung and left desolate, and without the help of God, we are left defenseless against these stings and wiles of Satan. One Woe is past and two more are to come! The 6th Trumpet and the 4 Angels of the Earth we released and for a year, a month, a day, and an hour prepared for this battle. Some say it is to come, yet I am saying it is taking place. See no more than I know what sin looks like, I don't know what a spiritual warfare looks like. Sure, I know mine, and you may say you know what it looks like. But, outside of the Word of the Lord, and Prayer, how much battle time do you have in? See, as David once said, you come in your armor and all your array, but I come in the name of the Lord, and this day I will take your head! If we try to fight any other way, we are defeated before starting. What does that mean, I cannot help but to believe that here, we are getting a glimpse into what is taking place when we are praying and in a spiritual battle. The 1/3 of men, is a reminder that Satan and his minions are not omnipresent, nor omnipotent. They are only able to cause problems where they are, see Luke 8 and the story of Legion, they begged Christ not to remove them from their territory where they already had a leg up. Later that day, that region asked Christ to leave! When we are not Christs' we too ask the presence of Him to leave, because in sin we are ashamed, and we are being defeated. We have just forgotten, Satan does not stop at a battle victory, but in devourment!

Chapter 10

Revelation 10:1 And I saw another mighty angel come down from heaven, clothed with a cloud: and a rainbow was upon his head, and his face was as it were the sun, and his feet as pillars of fire:

Revelation 10:2 And he had in his hand a little book open: and he set his right foot upon the sea, and his left foot on the earth,

Revelation 10:3 And cried with a loud voice, as when a lion roareth: and when he had cried, seven thunders uttered their voices.

Revelation 10:4 And when the seven thunders had uttered their voices, I was about to write: and I heard a voice from heaven saying unto me, Seal up those things which the seven thunders uttered, and write them not.

Revelation 10:5 And the angel which I saw stand upon the sea and upon the earth lifted up his hand to heaven,

Revelation 10:6 And sware by him that liveth for ever and ever, who created heaven, and the things that therein are, and the earth, and the things that therein are, and the sea, and the things which are therein, that there should be time no longer:

Revelation 10:7 But in the days of the voice of the seventh angel, when he shall begin to sound, the mystery of God should be finished, as he hath declared to his servants the prophets.

Revelation 10:8 And the voice which I heard from heaven spake unto me again, and said, Go and take the little book which is open in the hand of the angel which standeth upon the sea and upon the earth.

Revelation 10:9 And I went unto the angel, and said unto him, Give me the little book. And he said unto me, Take it, and eat it up; and it shall make thy belly bitter, but it shall be in thy mouth sweet as honey.

Revelation 10:10 And I took the little book out of the angel's hand, and ate it up; and it was in my mouth sweet as honey: and as soon as I had eaten it, my belly was bitter.

Revelation 10:11 And he said unto me, Thou must prophesy again before many peoples, and nations, and tongues, and kings.

John sees this mighty angel, and it is quite easy to suspect he is also about to blow a trumpet. I mean, let's be honest we all know it is coming from Corinthians, right? Yet, we get a curve ball here, a little book, a loud cry, and thundering's from the heavens. Seems, like the sounds that were cast out of that Censer, doesn't it? Could this be the beginning of the sounds of victory? The battle that has been fought over? John is about to tell us when he is told to shut the book and stop writing. He is on the other hand allowed to go and visit this angel, and a voice from heaven has told him to take the book. John eats as he is commanded, in what could possibly be to first signs of judgement. I believe the book was the word in faith, but from the book what is sweet to taste and bitter inside? Judgement. What have the martyrs been praying for? Judgement. What do we often declare we want to see at the end? Judgement. Oh, how sweet, to see it coming and to have the first tastes of watching it handed out, but when you have to digest it and you to must face judgement? Maybe you live better than I, but it is certainly something I am not looking forward to having to swallow. Now, that said, don't forget how this started in chapter 10, that loud roaring! Sounds like we are about to see some signs of Victory!

Chapter 11

Revelation 11:1 And there was given me a reed like unto a rod: and the angel stood, saying, Rise, and measure the temple of God, and the altar, and them that worship therein.

Revelation 11:2 But the court which is without the temple leave out, and measure it not; for it is given unto the Gentiles: and the holy city shall they tread under foot forty and two months.

Revelation 11:3 And I will give power unto my two witnesses, and they shall prophesy a thousand two hundred and threescore days, clothed in sackcloth.

Revelation 11:4 These are the two olive trees, and the two candlesticks standing before the God of the earth.

Revelation 11:5 And if any man will hurt them, fire proceedeth out of their mouth, and devoureth their enemies: and if any man will hurt them, he must in this manner be killed.

Revelation 11:6 These have power to shut heaven, that it rain not in the days of their prophecy: and have power over waters to turn them to blood, and to smite the earth with all plagues, as often as they will.

Revelation 11:7 And when they shall have finished their testimony, the beast that ascendeth out of the bottomless pit shall make war against them, and shall overcome them, and kill them.

One word in the beginning of this chapter, once again leads me to seeing a past tense and not a future one. That word, Gentiles. Now wait a minute, I know that the Gentiles are still non-Jews and sitting here typing this I would be considered one. This isn't a negative connotation that the Gentiles will tread the holy city underfoot, rather a reminder that they have a place in God's holy city. Let's not forget if we are moving futuristically in your mind what is about to be said from God. They shall be my people, I will be their God, and shall wipe the tears from their eyes. God isn't seeing a different sect of people; he is seeing the gathering of his Son's bride!

Oh but the witnesses, who are they? What groups are they? Many questions raise as to whom they are, but I want to ask you what are they doing? Let's be reminded of the passage, go unto the highways and the hedges and bid them to come that my house may be filled. They are human, given power over their earthly enemies, but not strong enough to overcome the evil one from the midst of the bottomless pit. There are still victories to come that only God can win, they are not even our fight!

Revelation 11:8 And their dead bodies shall lie in the street of the great city, which spiritually is called Sodom and Egypt, where also our Lord was crucified.

Revelation 11:9 And they of the people and kindreds and tongues and nations shall see their dead bodies three days and an half, and shall not suffer their dead bodies to be put in graves.

Revelation 11:10 And they that dwell upon the earth shall rejoice over them, and make merry, and shall send gifts one to another; because these two prophets tormented them that dwelt on the earth.

Revelation 11:11 And after three days and an half the spirit of life from God entered into them, and they stood upon their feet; and great fear fell upon them which saw them.

Revelation 11:12 And they heard a great voice from heaven saying unto them, Come up hither. And they ascended up to heaven in a cloud; and their enemies beheld them.

Revelation 11:13 And the same hour was there a great earthquake, and the tenth part of the city fell, and in the earthquake were slain of men seven thousand: and the remnant were affrighted, and gave glory to the God of heaven.

Evil is running this land, yes both today, and in this scripture. We see that as the prophets, are offering hope and torment is what is being seen from the world. So much so that no one cares to bury the witnesses yet walking by them are reminded of the peace that, the world thinks it is receiving. I don't have the answers for the time period and will not venture into that at this time, but Victory enters back into them in the spirt of life from God! They rise from the death sleep they were in, and ascend in a cloud as Christ did so, with their enemies beholding them. A small shaking from God, and a tenth die, and the remaining were affrightened and gave glory to God. Wait, wasn't that what the witnesses were working for to start with?

Revelation 11:14 The second woe is past; and, behold, the third woe cometh quickly.

Revelation 11:15 And the seventh angel sounded; and there were great voices in heaven, saying, The kingdoms of this world are become the kingdoms of our Lord, and of his Christ; and he shall reign for ever and ever.

Revelation 11:16 And the four and twenty elders, which sat before God on their seats, fell upon their faces, and worshipped God,

Revelation 11:17 Saying, We give thee thanks, O LORD God Almighty, which art, and wast, and art to come; because thou hast taken to thee thy great power, and hast reigned.

Revelation 11:18 And the nations were angry, and thy wrath is come, and the time of the dead, that they should be judged, and that thou shouldest give reward unto thy servants the prophets, and to the saints, and them that fear thy name, small and great; and shouldest destroy them which destroy the earth.

Revelation 11:19 And the temple of God was opened in heaven, and there was seen in his temple the ark of his testament: and there were lightnings, and voices, and thunderings, and an earthquake, and great hail.

Their death, the second woe is past now! See a woe isn't the end all be all, its just a woe! The kingdoms of the world are becoming the kingdoms of God is the cry! Victory is reigning, we are again coming to the place of judgement! This time around John, has eaten the book, it has become personal and real to him, even more so than ever before. The Temple is opened in Heaven, as Hebrews said It was therefore necessary that the patterns of the things in the heavens should be purified with these, but the heavenly things themselves with better sacrifices than these. Heb 9:23 What were these things? Sacrifices of blood for the remission of sins. Make no mistake Victory is fast approaching, but the time is not yet!

Chapter 12

Revelation 12:1 And there appeared a great wonder in heaven; a woman clothed with the sun, and the moon under her feet, and upon her head a crown of twelve stars:

Revelation 12:2 And she being with child cried, travailing in birth, and pained to be delivered.

Revelation 12:3 And there appeared another wonder in heaven; and behold a great red dragon, having seven heads and ten horns, and seven crowns upon his heads.

Revelation 12:4 And his tail drew the third part of the stars of heaven, and did cast them to the earth: and the dragon stood before the woman which was ready to be delivered, for to devour her child as soon as it was born.

Revelation 12:5 And she brought forth a man child, who was to rule all nations with a rod of iron: and her child was caught up unto God, and to his throne.

Revelation 12:6 And the woman fled into the wilderness, where she hath a place prepared of God, that they should feed her there a thousand two hundred and threescore days.

Revelation 12:7 And there was war in heaven: Michael and his angels fought against the dragon; and the dragon fought and his angels,

Revelation 12:8 And prevailed not; neither was their place found any more in heaven.

Revelation 12:9 And the great dragon was cast out, that old serpent, called the Devil, and Satan, which deceiveth the whole world: he was cast out into the earth, and his angels were cast out with him.

Revelation 12:10 And I heard a loud voice saying in heaven, Now is come salvation, and strength, and the kingdom of our God, and the power of his Christ: for the accuser of our brethren is cast down, which accused them before our God day and night.

Revelation 12:11 And they overcame him by the blood of the Lamb, and by the word of their testimony; and they loved not their lives unto the death.

Revelation 12:12 Therefore rejoice, ye heavens, and ye that dwell in them. Woe to the inhabiters of the earth and of the sea! for the devil is come down unto you, having great wrath, because he knoweth that he hath but a short time.

Revelation 12:13 And when the dragon saw that he was cast unto the earth, he persecuted the woman which brought forth the man child.

Revelation 12:14 And to the woman were given two wings of a great eagle, that she might fly into the wilderness, into her place, where she is nourished for a time, and times, and half a time, from the face of the serpent.

Revelation 12:15 And the serpent cast out of his mouth water as a flood after the woman, that he might cause her to be carried away of the flood.

Revelation 12:16 And the earth helped the woman, and the earth opened her mouth, and swallowed up the flood which the dragon cast out of his mouth.

Revelation 12:17 And the dragon was wroth with the woman, and went to make war with the remnant of her seed, which keep the commandments of God, and have the testimony of Jesus Christ.

A woman, a man child, the dragon, and a battle! Birth, deserts, floods, and wilderness! All these are hard to find in the Bible, if you are looking for them physically. Now, it would take a book to try to break everything in this down, and the assumption that one would understand it all. (I don't) I will, however, try to help you see the path that I see, and encourage you to study this out for yourself.

Many say the woman is Mary, and the child is Christ. This is not saying they are wrong; it is saying maybe it's a little more than that. The birth I believe was set from the foundation of the world, yet I also see so many times that God tried to allow his people to follow him without Christ's sacrifice. Then we have things like, the golden calf, Israel wanting a king, Israel defying their king, David and Bathsheba, the Old Covenant. All these required, man to constantly make the right decision to commit to God and deny self. Each prove in its own way the failure of man to be able to fulfill that. God provided way after way for man to choose Him as God, and man found way after way to destroy that relationship. The only remaining option was to put a plan of forgiveness, and Salvation in place in which man didn't hold the key to it. That plan was the supreme sacrifice of Christ! While Christ left his deity and overcame sin of this world as a man and offered himself a sacrifice for our sins. He also took the part of me working and keeping that out, all that is left for me if believing and trusting. We cannot cheat this sacrifice system, we cannot change it, improve it, we can only accept it or deny it.

Okay, now that we have that said, this dragon is Satan, and the removal of him from heaven. We find in Job, that Satan is already in the earth, so this must have taken place before Mary. That said and stay with me a minute in this. Luke 3 is the baptism of Christ, and the second listed genealogy of Christ. If you compare Luke 3 with Matthew 1 genealogies, you will notice a lot of differences. Matthew 1 is clearly the line of Joseph, the supposed father of Christ, Luke 3 then is not. The only remaining option for Christ's ancestors, is through his mother Mary. Luke 3 is also the only genealogy, that we have tracing back to Adam, which is listed as the Son of God. All this together, with Genesis 3 being the first sin of man in the garden, and the beginning of strife between woman's seed and the serpent/dragon, leads me to believe John is seeing all things laid out before him. How that God through history has protected this seed, the same one that we trace through Luke 3, the seed of Christ that began, with Adam and Eve.

I hope you see where it seems this is headed, through sin, woman and her seed were pressed out of the garden, into the wilderness of this world. The flood has been the continual outpouring of sinful attempts to destroy the bloodline of this seed, and the prevention of Christ's birth. We are here folks, as Paul said in Romans, we are heirs and joint heirs with Christ, we are a part of this seed through our faith in Christ. It is only through faith, through obedience in God's commandments, and the Testimony of Christ, that we are able to overcome this flood and see victory over the sin. All that said, I do not disagree this is Mary, just that is don't start with Mary. It starts with attempt to destroy Mary, before she would have a chance to accept from God, the opportunity to be the mother of Christ our Savior.

Chapter 13

Revelation 13:1 And I stood upon the sand of the sea, and saw a beast rise up out of the sea, having seven heads and ten horns, and upon his horns ten crowns, and upon his heads the name of blasphemy.

Revelation 13:2 And the beast which I saw was like unto a leopard, and his feet were as the feet of a bear, and his mouth as the mouth of a lion: and the dragon gave him his power, and his seat, and great authority.

Revelation 13:3 And I saw one of his heads as it were wounded to death; and his deadly wound was healed: and all the world wondered after the beast.

Revelation 13:4 And they worshipped the dragon which gave power unto the beast: and they worshipped the beast, saying, Who is like unto the beast? who is able to make war with him?

Revelation 13:5 And there was given unto him a mouth speaking great things and blasphemies; and power was given unto him to continue forty and two months.

Revelation 13:6 And he opened his mouth in blasphemy against God, to blaspheme his name, and his tabernacle, and them that dwell in heaven.

Revelation 13:7 And it was given unto him to make war with the saints, and to overcome them: and power was given him over all kindreds, and tongues, and nations.

Revelation 13:8 And all that dwell upon the earth shall worship him, whose names are not written in the book of life of the Lamb slain from the foundation of the world.

Revelation 13:9 If any man have an ear, let him hear.

Revelation 13:10 He that leadeth into captivity shall go into captivity: he that killeth with the sword must be killed with the sword. Here is the patience and the faith of the saints.

Let's pause here for a minute and take a recap of verses 1-10, before we see a change in direction. We are in the midst it seems of a recap of what has taken place thus far. From Chapter 12:1 – 14, we are seeing a rundown again of what has been taking place since chapter 4. I love the descriptions that John uses for these beasts in chapter 13, yet I don't want to get to caught up in appearances. Instead, allow us to look at what these beasts are doing. John himself makes that a point in verses 3-4 telling us the world is in wonder of this beast, and they are asking Who is like unto the beast? You may want to dig further into one coming from the sea and one coming from the land and make some determinations as to why. I only want to point out now on that fact, that there is a day coming when one foot will be placed on the sea, and one on the land declaring time shall be no more. That places both under the feet of the Victor, and the point of the Book again is to get you to choose the side of Victory!

Don't be in awe of the description, leopards, and bear feet, and 7 heads. (I am not belittling this in anyway,) yet I am saying that isn't the importance. You may be into some crazy looking beast appearing, and that is completely fine. Yet, through the Bible we have seen Satan, Demons, his angels, and followers, and none have appeared in any such manner. Why then is John seeing these this way? I believe it is for their purpose more so than for their appearing. See in short, this is a helper to Satan, look at what he is doing with blasphemies. Against God, his name, his tabernacle, and those in heaven. Yet again before we jump to far into the future, I think we are recapping. I offer the question again, what does sin and it's temptation look like in physicality? Where does it come from, is Satan is described as the god of this world? I would venture to say, it looks anyway it needs to in effort to steal your attention. It comes from anywhere that Satan can get a foot in, sea and land cover the entirety of the earth. The purpose of this beast is to overcome the Saints of the earth. Currently that is US! This form of Satan had a deadly wound on one of its heads, yet it has been healed. How is this? I believe it is what God was talking about in the beginning, with the seed bruising/wounding satan's head. How was it wounded? By, the work of the cross. So why then did it heal? That is the patience and the faith of the saints that was being talked about. As the Saints of old waited for the coming Messiah, that would bring Salvation to a world whom of itself was not able to overcome this beast. But what Christ did was done in the form a man! It was Him wounding this beast with living a perfect life, free from sin and failure. But man alone, even Christ in flesh was not enough to do away with Satan forever. It wounded him, Christ brought hope into a hopeless world, but in his return, he is coming not as a man, but as God's Holy Son for destruction.

Revelation 13:11 And I beheld another beast coming up out of the earth; and he had two horns like a lamb, and he spake as a dragon.

Revelation 13:12 And he exerciseth all the power of the first beast before him, and causeth the earth and them which dwell therein to worship the first beast, whose deadly wound was healed.

Revelation 13:13 And he doeth great wonders, so that he maketh fire come down from heaven on the earth in the sight of men,

Revelation 13:14 And deceiveth them that dwell on the earth by the means of those miracles which he had power to do in the sight of the beast; saying to them that dwell on the earth, that they should make an image to the beast, which had the wound by a sword, and did live.

Revelation 13:15 And he had power to give life unto the image of the beast, that the image of the beast should both speak, and cause that as many as would not worship the image of the beast should be killed.

Revelation 13:16 And he causeth all, both small and great, rich and poor, free and bond, to receive a mark in their right hand, or in their foreheads:

Revelation 13:17 And that no man might buy or sell, save he that had the mark, or the name of the beast, or the number of his name.

Revelation 13:18 Here is wisdom. Let him that hath understanding count the number of the beast: for it is the number of a man; and his number is Six hundred threescore and six.

Now, the second beast from land, more of the same as the first that was wounded. The first beast was enough to lead astray those who were not believers, and waged war on those who were. But now those believers have a risen Savior. They have direct access to all power in heaven and in earth. Christ has taken away the power of the beast of this world. That is why the second is leaning on the image of the first beast. Wanting to remind the world of the former power that once belonged to him, when no man could overcome sin. But, now through the grace of God, all who believe may overcome him UNLESS. .... Unless they are convinced that without the beast they can't live a successful life. Don't you find it terrifying that sin is an empty sack of promises of success. If you

want to fit in, you must buy and sell in sin. If you want to suc-
ceed, using sin is the only way. It is the message that is being sent
to us and our children everyday of our lives. Some even from so
called churches and ministers of god. In the television, through the
radio, in the songs we hear, and the education we are given. To be
a good human, you have to turn from the Salvation of the Lord,
you must be accepting and welcoming. Oh, what a tangled weave
of lies this second beast is pouring upon the world, and upon the
saints that will believe it. It isn't a new story, it's Satan, offering
fulfillment in every way outside of Christ.

Chapter 14

Revelation 14:1 And I looked, and, lo, a Lamb stood on the mount Sion, and with him an hundred forty and four thousand, having his Father's name written in their foreheads.

Revelation 14:2 And I heard a voice from heaven, as the voice of many waters, and as the voice of a great thunder: and I heard the voice of harpers harping with their harps:

Revelation 14:3 And they sung as it were a new song before the throne, and before the four beasts, and the elders: and no man could learn that song but the hundred and forty and four thousand, which were redeemed from the earth.

Revelation 14:4 These are they which were not defiled with women; for they are virgins. These are they which follow the Lamb whithersoever he goeth. These were redeemed from among men, being the firstfruits unto God and to the Lamb.

Revelation 14:5 And in their mouth was found no guile: for they are without fault before the throne of God.

Welcome The Lamb of God, as John said which taketh away the sins of the world. John looks, and lo, Standing is the Lamb. Notice unlike the beasts in chapter 13, he didn't rise, or come down, or appear. But he is just there and he is Standing. Why is the Lamb standing? Because, He is Victorious, and with him this 144,000 which we read about earlier. With them, the song of the redeemed! This number that is so disputed, are the firstfruits of the Resurrection, meaning? They had to be deceased before the Resurrection of the Lamb.

This is a perfect picture of God; in that we are often crying out for God to come and help us. Asking for Him, to go somewhere and work. But he is not like the beasts, He is the almighty God, and He does not have to go anywhere. He does not have to come anywhere. He is God. He is just there!

Revelation 14:6 And I saw another angel fly in the midst of heaven, having the everlasting gospel to preach unto them that dwell on the earth, and to every nation, and kindred, and tongue, and people,

Revelation 14:7 Saying with a loud voice, Fear God, and give glory to him; for the hour of his judgment is come: and worship him that made heaven, and earth, and the sea, and the fountains of waters.

Revelation 14:8 And there followed another angel, saying, Babylon is fallen, is fallen, that great city, because she made all nations drink of the wine of the wrath of her fornication.

Revelation 14:9 And the third angel followed them, saying with a loud voice, If any man worship the beast and his image, and receive his mark in his forehead, or in his hand,

Revelation 14:10 The same shall drink of the wine of the wrath of God, which is poured out without mixture into the cup of his indignation; and he shall be tormented with fire and brimstone in the presence of the holy angels, and in the presence of the Lamb:

Revelation 14:11 And the smoke of their torment ascendeth up for ever and ever: and they have no rest day nor night, who worship the beast and his image, and whosoever receiveth the mark of his name.

Revelation 14:12 Here is the patience of the saints: here are they that keep the commandments of God, and the faith of Jesus.

Revelation 14:13 And I heard a voice from heaven saying unto me, Write, Blessed are the dead which die in the Lord from henceforth: Yea, saith the Spirit, that they may rest from their labours; and their works do follow them.

Here is what the martyrs have been crying out for. Here is what John tasted when he ate that little book. Here is the sweet in the mouth and the bitter in the belly. Here is Judgement. The angel is carrying the eternal gospel bringing it to the earth. Proclaiming

that we should fear God, for his eternal judgement is come. Baby-
lon has fallen! That great city that was a strength of sin.

This judgement of God, notice without effort has brought destruc-
tion to the world that has followed the blasphemies, of the beast.
The world that has been selling sin and proclaiming it as truth.
This message is clear in the judgment of God, and it is laid out
as the proclamation of judgement. While destruction and death
are coming to sin, and its strongholds. In the same judgement, is
coming blessings, and rest to the saints that have been patient and
waited upon the Lord. Hold fast! There is coming a judgement,
we will all stand condemned before a Holy and Just God. Not
letting go of the hand of the Lord, is the only way to overcome that
condemnation, and find the blessing, and rest of God!

Revelation 14:14 And I looked, and behold a white cloud,
and upon the cloud one sat like unto the Son of man, having
on his head a golden crown, and in his hand a sharp sickle.

Revelation 14:15 And another angel came out of the temple,
crying with a loud voice to him that sat on the cloud, Thrust
in thy sickle, and reap: for the time is come for thee to reap;
for the harvest of the earth is ripe.

Revelation 14:16 And he that sat on the cloud thrust in his
sickle on the earth; and the earth was reaped.

Revelation 14:17 And another angel came out of the temple
which is in heaven, he also having a sharp sickle.

Revelation 14:18 And another angel came out from the altar, which had power over fire; and cried with a loud cry to him that had the sharp sickle, saying, Thrust in thy sharp sickle, and gather the clusters of the vine of the earth; for her grapes are fully ripe.

Revelation 14:19 And the angel thrust in his sickle into the earth, and gathered the vine of the earth, and cast it into the great winepress of the wrath of God.

Revelation 14:20 And the winepress was trodden without the city, and blood came out of the winepress, even unto the horse bridles, by the space of a thousand and six hundred furlongs.

There is without question, a day coming in every life when we take our last breath. Funerals are a real part of our life, and while in the midst of a funeral, we see the sadness, and the grief. As we live on past the initial hurt and grief, we are reminded of the certainty of life after death. All the same, there is coming a day, when an end to the earth is coming. When for the last time we all, will no longer worry about the tasks at hand. We all will not have to trudge one foot in front of the other, no worry about our shortcomings and failures. These last few verses are a depiction of that time. When, all the life in the earth is brought forth before God. When we like grapes, have the shell removed from our life, and the meat of what we are is pressed. The truth of our inner being is shown forth, naked and true before a Righteous God. John depicts this in a very matter of fact way, seeing the sickle brought forth, and every life reacting the same. No one will escape this day, or this time.

Chapter 15

Revelation 15:1 And I saw another sign in heaven, great and marvellous, seven angels having the seven last plagues; for in them is filled up the wrath of God.

Revelation 15:2 And I saw as it were a sea of glass mingled with fire: and them that had gotten the victory over the beast, and over his image, and over his mark, and over the number of his name, stand on the sea of glass, having the harps of God.

Revelation 15:3 And they sing the song of Moses the servant of God, and the song of the Lamb, saying, Great and marvellous are thy works, Lord God Almighty; just and true are thy ways, thou King of saints.

Revelation 15:4 Who shall not fear thee, O Lord, and glorify thy name? for thou only art holy: for all nations shall come and worship before thee; for thy judgments are made manifest.

Revelation 15:5 And after that I looked, and, behold, the temple of the tabernacle of the testimony in heaven was opened:

Revelation 15:6 And the seven angels came out of the temple, having the seven plagues, clothed in pure and white linen, and having their breasts girded with golden girdles.

Revelation 15:7 And one of the four beasts gave unto the seven angels seven golden vials full of the wrath of God, who liveth for ever and ever.

Revelation 15:8 And the temple was filled with smoke from the glory of God, and from his power; and no man was able to enter into the temple, till the seven plagues of the seven angels were fulfilled.

I am not sure if you have been paying attention over the past few chapters, but I wanted to point something out really quick as we start discussion on the 15th Chapter. Did you notice that John hasn't heard much recently? It was Chapter 12 verse 10 the last time John heard, but he has been doing a lot of seeing. Remember over the past few chapters, I told you we were recapping? Well, John is remembering things he has heard, and seen and is now watching those play out in front of him. Now, we have heard of judgement all of our lives, whether in the courts, on the playground, or in church. It has been spoken about and talked about, even threatened at times. Let me say though that judgement has never been heard! John, I believe, has seen in this vision through

15 chapters, times that judgment of God has been issued through time. Judgement can be seen, it can be witnessed, it can be felt, but you can not hear it. That is because judgement is an action, and while we remember it is bitter when it falls on us. We see here a picture of the beauty, of God's judgement, the worship and praise that fills the temple before we begin to see it poured out on the earth.

Notice with me as this chapter starts, along with at other times before judgement starts. There is something that happens. Do you see it? Read verses 1 and 2 again quickly, its there, nay they are there. God has NEVER poured out his judgement, in a fashion of anger as we do. We are so enraged oftentimes when we are trying to hand it out, and we hurt those that we love. Not God, he always makes mention of the believers, He always locates them. God always locates YOU, before he beings to allow his wrath to fall. Here is no different, John first sees the believers, the overcomers, those who have held on patiently, and they are safe! They have their harps, praise be to know we finally take them out of the willows, and this time to play them and sing praises for eternity. They sing the song of Moses (Deuteronomy chapter 32) a song filled with praise to God's faithfulness and power. The song of the Lamb, true are his ways, truth is the hand holder of redemption and righteousness. Once they are located, and the praises are being sung, the vials are handed out. These vials, or bowls, are the same kind that are filled with the prayers of saints and offered before God. Yet, these have been entrusted to one of the beasts at the alter of God, and the beast is handing them to the angels, to be poured on the earth. With only one thing left to do, God's glory fills the temple, and his power is being manifest, and no one can enter the temple. Why? Not until the wrath is finished being poured on the earth. When God at any time in the scripture, has poured out his wrath, during that time. It is judgement. No more bowing and pleading your case, no more time to say wait I was going to change. Not another moment, to persuade, just as in the courts of law. The prosecution and defense have made their cases, the witnesses have spoken, and nothing else is to be said. It is time to see judgement.

Chapter 16

Revelation 16:1 And I heard a great voice out of the temple saying to the seven angels, Go your ways, and pour out the vials of the wrath of God upon the earth.

Revelation 16:2 And the first went, and poured out his vial upon the earth; and there fell a noisome and grievous sore upon the men which had the mark of the beast, and upon them which worshipped his image.

Revelation 16:3 And the second angel poured out his vial upon the sea; and it became as the blood of a dead man: and every living soul died in the sea.

Revelation 16:4 And the third angel poured out his vial upon the rivers and fountains of waters; and they became blood.

Revelation 16:5 And I heard the angel of the waters say, Thou art righteous, O Lord, which art, and wast, and shalt be, because thou hast judged thus.

Revelation 16:6 For they have shed the blood of saints and prophets, and thou hast given them blood to drink; for they are worthy.

Revelation 16:7 And I heard another out of the altar say, Even so, Lord God Almighty, true and righteous are thy judgments.

Revelation 16:8 And the fourth angel poured out his vial upon the sun; and power was given unto him to scorch men with fire.

Revelation 16:9 And men were scorched with great heat, and blasphemed the name of God, which hath power over these plagues: and they repented not to give him glory.

Revelation 16:10 And the fifth angel poured out his vial upon the seat of the beast; and his kingdom was full of darkness; and they gnawed their tongues for pain,

Revelation 16:11 And blasphemed the God of heaven because of their pains and their sores, and repented not of their deeds.

Revelation 16:12 And the sixth angel poured out his vial upon the great river Euphrates; and the water thereof was dried up, that the way of the kings of the east might be prepared.

Revelation 16:13 And I saw three unclean spirits like frogs come out of the mouth of the dragon, and out of the mouth of the beast, and out of the mouth of the false prophet.

Revelation 16:14 For they are the spirits of devils, working miracles, which go forth unto the kings of the earth and of the whole world, to gather them to the battle of that great day of God Almighty.

Revelation 16:15 Behold, I come as a thief. Blessed is he that watcheth, and keepeth his garments, lest he walk naked, and they see his shame.

Revelation 16:16 And he gathered them together into a place called in the Hebrew tongue Armageddon.

Revelation 16:17 And the seventh angel poured out his vial into the air; and there came a great voice out of the temple of heaven, from the throne, saying, It is done.

Revelation 16:18 And there were voices, and thunders, and lightnings; and there was a great earthquake, such as was not since men were upon the earth, so mighty an earthquake, and so great.

Revelation 16:19 And the great city was divided into three parts, and the cities of the nations fell: and great Babylon came in remembrance before God, to give unto her the cup of the wine of the fierceness of his wrath.

Revelation 16:20 And every island fled away, and the mountains were not found.

Revelation 16:21 And there fell upon men a great hail out of heaven, every stone about the weight of a talent: and men blasphemed God because of the plague of the hail; for the plague thereof was exceeding great.

A look into judgement, once again something that is so often spoken of as some event that is to come. From sores to bloody waters, to heat from the sun scorching men, darkness, the water of the Euphrates drying up, then finally the earthquake and hail falling. One thing to point in the ideology of it all to come, is that the only plague, that is mentioned continually is the Euphrates drying up. Again, let me say before moving on, I am not the final authority on this book, nor any biblical writing, as a matter of fact, I do not feel that I have any hidden insight on this scripture. That said, I do have some questions. If this is to come, and this is going to lead to as many say, a literal battle in the valley of Armageddon, we are then saying that one of two things is going to happen. 1.) God is going to remove all free will and force every king of every nation to come together in battle. The same nations that are here now, the same ones that continually cheat, back stab and war with one another. The same that claim they are peaceful, and the ones who want to be known as warlords. The ones who can not sit together and work with one another to keep their people from starving. These men are going to come together, because a river went dry? 2.) Is the opposite of one, if God does not remove free will, they are going to do this all on their own accord? They are going to choose that the one time in all of living to fight together, is against the God of the Universe. With all the results, already being foretold. Knowing the massacre that is told to occur?

Now, for me, just for me. I can not believe it is number 1. 16:11 just told us men would not repent of their deeds! They still have that choice and are still making the wrong one. So that leads to the answer being that all leaders are going to willingly come together, know what has been told? OK, honestly, I just can't get on board with it. (I am not saying they are wrong for thinking so, greater men than I believe that whole heartedly.) I am just saying I am not convinced, that this is all setting up to be one final show-down to see who the Ruler is. WE KNOW! We know that God reigns supreme, we have seen Christ defeat Satan as a man, when he overcame the temptations of Satan directly. We have seen, him victorious as a man, crying My God, My God, why hast thou forsaken me? And in turn giving his life to God the Father, and God ACCEPTED his SON! We seen Satan defeated spiritually, being cast down for wanting to be worshipped instead of worshipping. What battle is there to really be won?

If you were to apply all of these vials/bowls being poured out upon the earth though as the trumpets, we sounded, and as the seals were being opened. If, you were to look through the portals of time, and see as John felt when he drank that bowl from the Angel sweet and bitter. If, one was to see all that and realize that God's judgement is not something that is to be determined, instead has already been made. If, you were to say believe that without Christ you will die and face the complete judgment of God and be cast away. Yet, if you would accept Christ, you still face that same judgement, (yes God is still fare to all, and all are still sinners) BUT you face it with the blood of his Son, who overcame and brought righteousness. We all face the same judge, the same judgement, we are all guilty, we are all failures, we have all lost the personal battles of sin in life and save Christ's pleading for us we all are hopeless. Then, you might see, that this judgement has always been. One might see, that sin has always plagued man this way, with pain, separation, darkness, gnashing of teeth on one another. One, might like I believe John did this day, see that Christ was far more important, and necessary in keeping us from God's judgement in our lives, that we have ever imagined.

Chapter 17

Revelation 17:1 And there came one of the seven angels which had the seven vials, and talked with me, saying unto me, Come hither; I will shew unto thee the judgment of the great whore that sitteth upon many waters:

Revelation 17:2 With whom the kings of the earth have committed fornication, and the inhabitants of the earth have been made drunk with the wine of her fornication.

Revelation 17:3 So he carried me away in the spirit into the wilderness: and I saw a woman sit upon a scarlet coloured beast, full of names of blasphemy, having seven heads and ten horns.

Revelation 17:4 And the woman was arrayed in purple and scarlet colour, and decked with gold and precious stones and pearls, having a golden cup in her hand full of abominations and filthiness of her fornication:

Revelation 17:5 And upon her forehead was a name written, MYSTERY, BABYLON THE GREAT, THE MOTHER OF HARLOTS AND ABOMINATIONS OF THE EARTH.

Revelation 17:6 And I saw the woman drunken with the blood of the saints, and with the blood of the martyrs of Jesus: and when I saw her, I wondered with great admiration.

Revelation 17:7 And the angel said unto me, Wherefore didst thou marvel? I will tell thee the mystery of the woman, and of the beast that carrieth her, which hath the seven heads and ten horns.

Revelation 17:8 The beast that thou sawest was, and is not; and shall ascend out of the bottomless pit, and go into perdition: and they that dwell on the earth shall wonder, whose names were not written in the book of life from the foundation of the world, when they behold the beast that was, and is not, and yet is.

Revelation 17:9 And here is the mind which hath wisdom. The seven heads are seven mountains, on which the woman sitteth.

Revelation 17:10 And there are seven kings: five are fallen, and one is, and the other is not yet come; and when he cometh, he must continue a short space.

Revelation 17:11 And the beast that was, and is not, even he is the eighth, and is of the seven, and goeth into perdition.

Revelation 17:12 And the ten horns which thou sawest are ten kings, which have received no kingdom as yet; but receive power as kings one hour with the beast.

Revelation 17:13 These have one mind, and shall give their power and strength unto the beast.

Revelation 17:14 These shall make war with the Lamb, and the Lamb shall overcome them: for he is Lord of lords, and King of kings: and they that are with him are called, and chosen, and faithful.

Revelation 17:15 And he saith unto me, The waters which thou sawest, where the whore sitteth, are peoples, and multitudes, and nations, and tongues.

Revelation 17:16 And the ten horns which thou sawest upon the beast, these shall hate the whore, and shall make her desolate and naked, and shall eat her flesh, and burn her with fire.

Revelation 17:17 For God hath put in their hearts to fulfil his will, and to agree, and give their kingdom unto the beast, until the words of God shall be fulfilled.

Revelation 17:18 And the woman which thou sawest is that great city, which reigneth over the kings of the earth.

There is something about a wedding, that makes even the grouchiest of humanity, if only for a moment inside smile. It's joining of lives and showing that togetherness is possible. It's used often in the Bible to show us lessons, and encouragement. It is used to identify those involved, it is always the honor of the one presiding, to for the first time introduce a new Mr. and Mrs. It was established and ordained of God, no matter how one may want to ar-

gue the case, (and this is not the time) you can not get away from the fact that marriage is biblical. We see through the scripture that the Church (believers) is/will be the Bride of Christ. There is a marriage supper coming soon, a celebration like none other.

Why start with marriage? Well, do you know that God's plan is perfect? Do you believe that the way he set things up is the right way? Do you believe that He put that in his word for us to know and follow? You need to realize this if you don't already, Satan and all the demons in Hell, they know that too, and believe, and they fear. As a matter of fact, if you study the ways of satan and how he is organized, you might find that his plans follow the same direction as God's plans ahhh let's say 85%. This mysterious woman, that we read about in chapter 17, this harlot. She is the mirrored part of the Bride of Christ. Except, she isn't a bride, see what I mean by 85%? Enough that is looks similar, one might try to say close enough, but its still denying the fullness of God! She has no name, don't be alarmed, what is the name of the Bride of Christ? This harlot is made up of those that have made a commitment in their lives to deny and blaspheme, just as believers have made a commitment to edify and uplift the name of God. That commitment has led many astray and cause as verse 14 says many to make war with the Lamb, yet we again are quick to see that the Lamb shall overcome them all.

While so many churches today are busy on Sunday morning complaining about the sin-filled world we live in, I have often wondered why they are not out making an invitation to come to an actual wedding. Not only to come and see, but to come and be a part of this wedding, to join and be a Bride of the highest? I was in a church back of this a bit, and every summer you could bet that someone would bring up the same point. Just north of the church was a set of ballfields, and they were full of kids playing ball, that point they made? It's a shame that families are making a god out of little league and denying God. I am in complete agreement with that statement, but the problem was, no one was ever willing to go along after church and make an effort to know and invite those families to church. As a church we are content with sitting and talking about the whoredoms of the world, but we are not willing to go shine light in those dark places to bring victory. See those with the Lamb in verse 14 were believers, chosen and faithful. God is still choosing to use the Church (chosen and faithful) to shine light into darkness, and when we as the Bride of Christ are not willing to fulfill that motherly role. Satan has a mirrored stand in, almost the same, but she is telling them to play on Sunday night when it is cooler as well as Sunday morning.

Chapter 18

Revelation 18:1 And after these things I saw another angel come down from heaven, having great power; and the earth was lightened with his glory.

Revelation 18:2 And he cried mightily with a strong voice, saying, Babylon the great is fallen, is fallen, and is become the habitation of devils, and the hold of every foul spirit, and a cage of every unclean and hateful bird.

Revelation 18:3 For all nations have drunk of the wine of the wrath of her fornication, and the kings of the earth have committed fornication with her, and the merchants of the earth are waxed rich through the abundance of her delicacies.

Revelation 18:4 And I heard another voice from heaven, saying, Come out of her, my people, that ye be not partakers of her sins, and that ye receive not of her plagues.

Revelation 18:5 For her sins have reached unto heaven, and God hath remembered her iniquities.

Revelation 18:6 Reward her even as she rewarded you, and double unto her double according to her works: in the cup which she hath filled fill to her double.

Revelation 18:7 How much she hath glorified herself, and lived deliciously, so much torment and sorrow give her: for she saith in her heart, I sit a queen, and am no widow, and shall see no sorrow.

Revelation 18:8 Therefore shall her plagues come in one day, death, and mourning, and famine; and she shall be utterly burned with fire: for strong is the Lord God who judgeth her.

Revelation 18:9 And the kings of the earth, who have committed fornication and lived deliciously with her, shall bewail her, and lament for her, when they shall see the smoke of her burning,

Revelation 18:10 Standing afar off for the fear of her torment, saying, Alas, alas that great city Babylon, that mighty city! for in one hour is thy judgment come.

Revelation 18:11 And the merchants of the earth shall weep and mourn over her; for no man buyeth their merchandise any more:

Revelation 18:12 The merchandise of gold, and silver, and precious stones, and of pearls, and fine linen, and purple, and silk, and scarlet, and all thyine wood, and all manner vessels of ivory, and all manner vessels of most precious wood, and of brass, and iron, and marble,

Revelation 18:13 And cinnamon, and odours, and ointments, and frankincense, and wine, and oil, and fine flour, and wheat, and beasts, and sheep, and horses, and chariots, and slaves, and souls of men.

Revelation 18:14 And the fruits that thy soul lusted after are departed from thee, and all things which were dainty and goodly are departed from thee, and thou shalt find them no more at all.

Revelation 18:15 The merchants of these things, which were made rich by her, shall stand afar off for the fear of her torment, weeping and wailing,

Revelation 18:16 And saying, Alas, alas that great city, that was clothed in fine linen, and purple, and scarlet, and decked with gold, and precious stones, and pearls!

Revelation 18:17 For in one hour so great riches is come to nought. And every shipmaster, and all the company in ships, and sailors, and as many as trade by sea, stood afar off,

Revelation 18:18 And cried when they saw the smoke of her burning, saying, What city is like unto this great city!

Revelation 18:19 And they cast dust on their heads, and cried, weeping and wailing, saying, Alas, alas that great city, wherein were made rich all that had ships in the sea by reason of her costliness! for in one hour is she made desolate.

Revelation 18:20 Rejoice over her, thou heaven, and ye holy apostles and prophets; for God hath avenged you on her.

Revelation 18:21 And a mighty angel took up a stone like a great millstone, and cast it into the sea, saying, Thus with violence shall that great city Babylon be thrown down, and shall be found no more at all.

Revelation 18:22 And the voice of harpers, and musicians, and of pipers, and trumpeters, shall be heard no more at all in thee; and no craftsman, of whatsoever craft he be, shall be found any more in thee; and the sound of a millstone shall be heard no more at all in thee;

Revelation 18:23 And the light of a candle shall shine no more at all in thee; and the voice of the bridegroom and of the bride shall be heard no more at all in thee: for thy merchants were the great men of the earth; for by thy sorceries were all nations deceived.

Revelation 18:24 And in her was found the blood of prophets, and of saints, and of all that were slain upon the earth.

Sin is so often a misused word, in my opinion, it is always looked at as a level of badness in someone's life. It is often made into a lifestyle, alcoholic, drug addict, whoremonger, etc. While we are often so busy, defining it, we are not as apt to be recognizing it in

*our lives. I believe Chapter 18 is the greatest example of recogniz-
ing sin, and seeing it torn apart once it is recognized. I am a true
believer that no one just wakes up and chooses to be a bad person.
Too often, we just complain about their habits, or way, and never
go to them with examples of how they are. When we do that person will try to make a change in their life. That is the way we are
with sin, we define it, we watch outward for it, but its hard to see
it in ourselves. When we miss it in ourselves, that is when we fall
victim to this chapter.*

*Babylon has been destroyed for years when this is written, yet it is
still known as the most sinful city that had been. Men still study
the great city of Babylon and all that is had to offer. It was a
merchant city, near ocean with great access. Many ports, and sellers of every type flogged there in hopes to make it big. Most were
successful in selling, but the problem was that it was known for
its thievery and cheating as well. Use of fake coins, unbalanced
scales, and such were ways that sellers would cheat both their
supplier, and their merchants. There is a celebration going on here
about its fall, not the physical fall of the city, but the sinful hold
fall that took place when Babylon fell. We see the ships offshore
watching it burn, people fleeing and not trying to help save it. It
was the livelihood of all of these people but had instilled in them
the selfishness of sin. They could have banned together and made
a difference, but not seeing their own sin, and seeing only their
benefit, they split and allowed it to fall quickly.*

This is what happens with us as we hang around sin, we first walk through, hiding our faces, wanting nothing, and just trying to get away. But, as we chose to not find another path and continue to walk through, we begin to look at what is being sold. "There is still pleasure in sin for a season" and soon enough we pick up an item. We take it home, and it doesn't burn the house down, so maybe it is not that bad. We look for something nicer, and slowly we begin to do more business in sin, than we do in prayer. Guilt comes, we know better! Yet, we can't just throw away what we have invested in it! So, we begin to sale what we have. It can not be that bad, nothing has really happened to us, right? I mean we are not like the other salesmen cheating folks, but we need to retrieve our investment. We forget that when we mess with sin, it is a loss. That's right a complete loss, you can't get back what you put in it, you can't clean yours up enough to make it right, and you can't get back the time you invested achieving it. Just like that, we are selling the same things we were before avoiding, because we spent to much time trying to identify what it was, and not realizing sin isn't an item. It's not a drink, a ballgame, the lake, a motorcycle. It isn't all these things we have bought; it is the time we have given in our lives placing them in front of God, and now selling sin is more important that living for God. That is what led to Babylon falling, and that is still what causes lives to fall out of fellowship with God today.

Chapter 19

Revelation 19:1 And after these things I heard a great voice of much people in heaven, saying, Alleluia; Salvation, and glory, and honour, and power, unto the Lord our God:

Revelation 19:2 For true and righteous are his judgments: for he hath judged the great whore, which did corrupt the earth with her fornication, and hath avenged the blood of his servants at her hand.

Revelation 19:3 And again they said, Alleluia And her smoke rose up for ever and ever.

Revelation 19:4 And the four and twenty elders and the four beasts fell down and worshipped God that sat on the throne, saying, Amen; Alleluia.

Revelation 19:5 And a voice came out of the throne, saying, Praise our God, all ye his servants, and ye that fear him, both small and great.

Revelation 19:6 And I heard as it were the voice of a great multitude, and as the voice of many waters, and as the voice of mighty thunderings, saying, Alleluia: for the Lord God omnipotent reigneth.

Revelation 19:7 Let us be glad and rejoice, and give honour to him: for the marriage of the Lamb is come, and his wife hath made herself ready.

Revelation 19:8 And to her was granted that she should be arrayed in fine linen, clean and white: for the fine linen is the righteousness of saints.

Revelation 19:9 And he saith unto me, Write, Blessed are they which are called unto the marriage supper of the Lamb. And he saith unto me, These are the true sayings of God.

Revelation 19:10 And I fell at his feet to worship him. And he said unto me, See thou do it not: I am thy fellowservant, and of thy brethren that have the testimony of Jesus: worship God: for the testimony of Jesus is the spirit of prophecy.

Revelation 19:11 And I saw heaven opened, and behold a white horse; and he that sat upon him was called Faithful and True, and in righteousness he doth judge and make war.

Revelation 19:12 His eyes were as a flame of fire, and on his head were many crowns; and he had a name written, that no man knew, but he himself.

Revelation 19:13 And he was clothed with a vesture dipped in blood: and his name is called The Word of God.

Revelation 19:14 And the armies which were in heaven followed him upon white horses, clothed in fine linen, white and clean.

Revelation 19:15 And out of his mouth goeth a sharp sword, that with it he should smite the nations: and he shall rule them with a rod of iron: and he treadeth the winepress of the fierceness and wrath of Almighty God.

Revelation 19:16 And he hath on his vesture and on his thigh a name written, KING OF KINGS, AND LORD OF LORDS.

There is an old saying about the winds of change are coming, and that is what is taking place in the first 15 verses here. The Lamb has completed all that is to be overcome, and Judgement has reigned out! Now, King of Kings and Lord of Lords, is coming to take his bride. See in biblical times, the couple didn't meet at the church on the wedding day, when the house was prepared, and the meal was ready, the bridegroom, left his home where the couple would stay. He went to the house of the bride, and there was only one thing on his mind, getting his Bride. She was done carrying water for her father's house, she was done sweeping his floors, and living for her father. The Bridegroom, came and took the Bride, and her family did the only thing they could do. They went to the supper to make preparation for the marriage. Christ has come now in superiority, to take his Bride and return to His Father's house where preparation has been made for them to live. That is the Christ we see here, His Kingship shown, Christ did not overcome the world and sin, to be seen as a meek and mild lowly Jesus, He is KING OF KINGS, and nothing is going to prevent him from claiming his Bride.

Revelation 19:17 And I saw an angel standing in the sun; and he cried with a loud voice, saying to all the fowls that fly in the midst of heaven, Come and gather yourselves together unto the supper of the great God;

Revelation 19:18 That ye may eat the flesh of kings, and the flesh of captains, and the flesh of mighty men, and the flesh of horses, and of them that sit on them, and the flesh of all men, both free and bond, both small and great.

Revelation 19:19 And I saw the beast, and the kings of the earth, and their armies, gathered together to make war against him that sat on the horse, and against his army.

Revelation 19:20 And the beast was taken, and with him the false prophet that wrought miracles before him, with which he deceived them that had received the mark of the beast, and them that worshipped his image. These both were cast alive into a lake of fire burning with brimstone.

Revelation 19:21 And the remnant were slain with the sword of him that sat upon the horse, which sword proceeded out of his mouth: and all the fowls were filled with their flesh.

This battle that so many have fussed over for years, was just laid out in 5 verses. Sin even the greatest of it can not be present in the place of a Holy God, that has overcome it. Again, I am not looking for some battle to be taking place, to prove Lordship over the earth, if so, how can he be titles KING OF KING and LORD of LORDS. This I believe is something that is taking place in that same twinkle of an eye that Paul spoke of. We will not prevent them which are asleep, we will lay off this mortality and in a that split-second, put-on immortality. At His appearing, I believe any that may have gathered to fight will likewise fall and see this change take place, and when this earth is claimed by the KING OF KINGS obtaining his bride, satan, the beast mentioned, and the false prophet will have no where to reside, as they can not be in the presence of King Jesus. This world is made ready for destruction, as each person is claimed as described in chapter 14 as the sickles were placed in the earth to reap. We all, everyone that has had breathe are about to stand in the Presence of the Mighty God.

Chapter 20

Revelation 20:1 And I saw an angel come down from heaven, having the key of the bottomless pit and a great chain in his hand.

Revelation 20:2 And he laid hold on the dragon, that old serpent, which is the Devil, and Satan, and bound him a thousand years,

Revelation 20:3 And cast him into the bottomless pit, and shut him up, and set a seal upon him, that he should deceive the nations no more, till the thousand years should be fulfilled: and after that he must be loosed a little season.

Revelation 20:4 And I saw thrones, and they sat upon them, and judgment was given unto them: and I saw the souls of them that were beheaded for the witness of Jesus, and for the word of God, and which had not worshipped the beast, neither his image, neither had received his mark upon their foreheads, or in their hands; and they lived and reigned with Christ a thousand years.

Revelation 20:5 But the rest of the dead lived not again until the thousand years were finished. This is the first resurrection.

Revelation 20:6 Blessed and holy is he that hath part in the first resurrection: on such the second death hath no power, but they shall be priests of God and of Christ, and shall reign with him a thousand years.

Revelation 20:7 And when the thousand years are expired, Satan shall be loosed out of his prison,

Revelation 20:8 And shall go out to deceive the nations which are in the four quarters of the earth, Gog, and Magog, to gather them together to battle: the number of whom is as the sand of the sea.

Revelation 20:9 And they went up on the breadth of the earth, and compassed the camp of the saints about, and the beloved city: and fire came down from God out of heaven, and devoured them.

Revelation 20:10 And the devil that deceived them was cast into the lake of fire and brimstone, where the beast and the false prophet are, and shall be tormented day and night for ever and ever.

Revelation 20:11 And I saw a great white throne, and him that sat on it, from whose face the earth and the heaven fled away; and there was found no place for them.

Revelation 20:12 And I saw the dead, small and great, stand before God; and the books were opened: and another book was opened, which is the book of life: and the dead were judged out of those things which were written in the books, according to their works.

Revelation 20:13 And the sea gave up the dead which were in it; and death and hell delivered up the dead which were in them: and they were judged every man according to their works.

Revelation 20:14 And death and hell were cast into the lake of fire. This is the second death.

Revelation 20:15 And whosoever was not found written in the book of life was cast into the lake of fire.

Now, life is over as we know it, and here comes the angel from heaven with the key of the pit. Much has been made about how Christ obtained them, I am going to tell you he did by overcoming the satan, that through death he was faithful and sinless. That is why at the name of Jesus, he must flee, the power that he was given in this earth was taken by Christ and that included the locks on the door if you will. And here is comes that bitter discussion that takes place so often on the mention of Christ reigning a thou-

sand years and satan being loosed. Can you read that last sentence one more time? If that holds, water you must believe that the loosening of satan has an affect on the power of Christ. My friend you must turn that around, it's the presence of Christ, the defeats satan!! This timeframe is mentioned 6 times all in chapter 20, some have said that is because Christ didn't know when he was here. My friend Christ was here in the beginning, and he simply laid aside his deity to face sin as a man because we couldn't, he didn't come dumber than he was, he came with the knowledge of the Father. He came with the knowledge of death by the cross as his purpose! To think that God would have hidden anything from his Son is to deny the fullness of the Trinity!

I want to say this if you are taking the number a thousand literal, the rest must be as well. In November of 2022 it was predicted the world population would reach 8 billion people! A world where overpopulation is a problem, feeding all the world has been an issue for years. Now, if there is a volunteer, would someone pick a beach, any beach, and count the sand for me there? Let me give you a start, there are about 6 million in a pound of dry sand! If we are talking literal here, then where are the people for the armies that are "the number of whom is as the sand of the sea" going to come from? Where are they going to gather in one place? Seeing that there is not a land mass to hold that number, it must be more than just in the moment. I want to present to you, that this has been part of an ongoing battle from the beginning of time once again. That, there is not just a one-time fight for the souls of man, but the daily it is waged and will be until the time of the Resurrection.

Now that we have been resurrected, we are placed before the great white throne, many refer to this as the great white throne judgement, again I am not arguing that I just feel that this book has been clear about the judgement of God. This is more of what we would call a sentencing! We have pled our case in our lives, we have chosen to try to be faithful and true, or to walk away from the gift of Life that was offered on the Cross. Its to late for a plea to change judgement on our lives! We are all GUILTY! Now, we are going to know what it is truly like to be thankful for the mercy of Christ, and the Gift of God that is eternal life through Jesus Christ our Lord. Whosoever is not found in the Book of Life, is cast into the fire, depart from me for I never knew you. What a horrific set of last words to hear, all because you refused to believe in Christ and trust in the work of the Cross!

Chapter 21

Revelation 21:1 And I saw a new heaven and a new earth: for the first heaven and the first earth were passed away; and there was no more sea.

Revelation 21:2 And I John saw the holy city, new Jerusalem, coming down from God out of heaven, prepared as a bride adorned for her husband.

Revelation 21:3 And I heard a great voice out of heaven saying, Behold, the tabernacle of God is with men, and he will dwell with them, and they shall be his people, and God himself shall be with them, and be their God.

Revelation 21:4 And God shall wipe away all tears from their eyes; and there shall be no more death, neither sorrow, nor crying, neither shall there be any more pain: for the former things are passed away.

Revelation 21:5 And he that sat upon the throne said, Behold, I make all things new. And he said unto me, Write: for these words are true and faithful.

Revelation 21:6 And he said unto me, It is done. I am Alpha and Omega, the beginning and the end. I will give unto him that is athirst of the fountain of the water of life freely.

Revelation 21:7 He that overcometh shall inherit all things; and I will be his God, and he shall be my son.

Revelation 21:8 But the fearful, and unbelieving, and the abominable, and murderers, and whoremongers, and sorcerers, and idolaters, and all liars, shall have their part in the lake which burneth with fire and brimstone: which is the second death.

Revelation 21:9 And there came unto me one of the seven angels which had the seven vials full of the seven last plagues, and talked with me, saying, Come hither, I will shew thee the bride, the Lamb's wife.

Revelation 21:10 And he carried me away in the spirit to a great and high mountain, and shewed me that great city, the holy Jerusalem, descending out of heaven from God,

Revelation 21:11 Having the glory of God: and her light was like unto a stone most precious, even like a jasper stone, clear as crystal;

Revelation 21:12 And had a wall great and high, and had twelve gates, and at the gates twelve angels, and names written thereon, which are the names of the twelve tribes of the children of Israel:

Revelation 21:13 On the east three gates; on the north three gates; on the south three gates; and on the west three gates.

Revelation 21:14 And the wall of the city had twelve foundations, and in them the names of the twelve apostles of the Lamb.

Revelation 21:15 And he that talked with me had a golden reed to measure the city, and the gates thereof, and the wall thereof.

Revelation 21:16 And the city lieth foursquare, and the length is as large as the breadth: and he measured the city with the reed, twelve thousand furlongs. The length and the breadth and the height of it are equal.

Revelation 21:17 And he measured the wall thereof, an hundred and forty and four cubits, according to the measure of a man, that is, of the angel.

Revelation 21:18 And the building of the wall of it was of jasper: and the city was pure gold, like unto clear glass.

Revelation 21:19 And the foundations of the wall of the city were garnished with all manner of precious stones. The first foundation was jasper; the second, sapphire; the third, a chalcedony; the fourth, an emerald;

Revelation 21:20 The fifth, sardonyx; the sixth, sardius; the seventh, chrysolyte; the eighth, beryl; the ninth, a topaz; the tenth, a chrysoprasus; the eleventh, a jacinth; the twelfth, an amethyst.

Revelation 21:21 And the twelve gates were twelve pearls: every several gate was of one pearl: and the street of the city was pure gold, as it were transparent glass.

Revelation 21:22 And I saw no temple therein: for the Lord God Almighty and the Lamb are the temple of it.

Revelation 21:23 And the city had no need of the sun, neither of the moon, to shine in it: for the glory of God did lighten it, and the Lamb is the light thereof.

Revelation 21:24 And the nations of them which are saved shall walk in the light of it: and the kings of the earth do bring their glory and honour into it.

Revelation 21:25 And the gates of it shall not be shut at all by day: for there shall be no night there.

Revelation 21:26 And they shall bring the glory and honour of the nations into it.

Revelation 21:27 And there shall in no wise enter into it any thing that defileth, neither whatsoever worketh abomination, or maketh a lie: but they which are written in the Lamb's book of life.

It is clearly done here; God has said so! The Marriage of the Lamb. The Victory that we have hoped for, longed for, prayed for. God has delivered in full every promise that has ever been made. What is there to say other than this, they shall in no wise enter in, but they which are written in the Lamb's Book of Life. This Book is no different than the other 65 in that its purpose is to draw you into a relationship with Christ Jesus. Now aside from that, let me say this. STOP! Take 15 minutes, and read this chapter again, and again, and again. God loves his people and there is a reward for those the diligently seek him! Praise be the name of the LORD!

Chapter 22

Revelation 22:1 And he shewed me a pure river of water of life, clear as crystal, proceeding out of the throne of God and of the Lamb.

Revelation 22:2 In the midst of the street of it, and on either side of the river, was there the tree of life, which bare twelve manner of fruits, and yielded her fruit every month: and the leaves of the tree were for the healing of the nations.

Revelation 22:3 And there shall be no more curse: but the throne of God and of the Lamb shall be in it; and his servants shall serve him:

Revelation 22:4 And they shall see his face; and his name shall be in their foreheads.

Revelation 22:5 And there shall be no night there; and they need no candle, neither light of the sun; for the Lord God giveth them light: and they shall reign for ever and ever.

While we are in the last chapter of the Book of Revelation, and we are reading about the glories of that great city, and so often we are looking for the return of Christ at this point. As well as we should, I am not convinced that after John, has seen this glorious sight and begins to close, that we should begin to close time. John is about to come to himself on Patmos, it will be the Lord's Day as it was 22 Chapters ago. He is just going to be a lot more informed that he has ever been.

Revelation 22:6 And he said unto me, These sayings are faithful and true: and the Lord God of the holy prophets sent his angel to shew unto his servants the things which must shortly be done.

Revelation 22:7 Behold, I come quickly: blessed is he that keepeth the sayings of the prophecy of this book.

Revelation 22:8 And I John saw these things, and heard them. And when I had heard and seen, I fell down to worship before the feet of the angel which shewed me these things.

Revelation 22:9 Then saith he unto me, See thou do it not: for I am thy fellowservant, and of thy brethren the prophets, and of them which keep the sayings of this book: worship God.

Revelation 22:10 And he saith unto me, Seal not the sayings of the prophecy of this book: for the time is at hand.

Revelation 22:11 He that is unjust, let him be unjust still: and he which is filthy, let him be filthy still: and he that is righteous, let him be righteous still: and he that is holy, let him be holy still.

Revelation 22:12 And, behold, I come quickly; and my reward is with me, to give every man according as his work shall be.

Revelation 22:13 I am Alpha and Omega, the beginning and the end, the first and the last.

Revelation 22:14 Blessed are they that do his commandments, that they may have right to the tree of life, and may enter in through the gates into the city.

Revelation 22:15 For without are dogs, and sorcerers, and whoremongers, and murderers, and idolaters, and whosoever loveth and maketh a lie.

Revelation 22:16 I Jesus have sent mine angel to testify unto you these things in the churches. I am the root and the offspring of David, and the bright and morning star.

Revelation 22:17 And the Spirit and the bride say, Come. And let him that heareth say, Come. And let him that is athirst come. And whosoever will, let him take the water of life freely.

Revelation 22:18 For I testify unto every man that heareth the words of the prophecy of this book, If any man shall add unto these things, God shall add unto him the plagues that are written in this book:

Revelation 22:19 And if any man shall take away from the words of the book of this prophecy, God shall take away his part out of the book of life, and out of the holy city, and from the things which are written in this book.

Revelation 22:20 He which testifieth these things saith, Surely I come quickly. Amen. Even so, come, Lord Jesus.

Revelation 22:21 The grace of our Lord Jesus Christ be with you all. Amen.

As I said, let's not write the end of the world just yet. There are some things that raise concern about doing so! For instance, verse 16, if we are complete and done, why is the angel being sent out? Why are the Spirit and the Bridegroom still saying come and take of the water of Life freely? Isn't that the message of today? Why, then was Jesus coming quickly? Why the warning if time is over? I am pressed to believe that John is seeing, preparation at the end, for what brought Hope, Judgement, and Victory to start with. A baby, about to be born in Bethlehem, as a Savior which is Christ the Lord. Let us be reminded of that HOPE

want to say again, I do not believe that I have special insight that others don't. I do not think this is the only way to view this book and enjoy discussions with scripture read folks about all the Bible. These are just some of my thoughts, hoping to press you to think, that together we may all grow and walk closer to Christ. I don't want you to think this is a complete in-depth look, as my feeble mind has only scratched the surface of what is in this book.

Thank you to Tammy Thompson, for encouraging and pushing me to complete this project. I am so grateful for Burem Church, and my Pastor and dear friend George "Fuzz" Bradley Jr., for the years that you have poured the word into my life and pressed me to study and be the best minister of the Word that I can be. To my family, who through this year, have always encouraged me to keep going, and not to quit, when quitting seemed so easy. I love each of you deeply, and hope that this encourages, helps, and opens your hearts and minds.

In Christ,
Jonathan Carver